REFORMING
GOVERNMENT

REFORMING GOVERNMENT

Daniel L. Feldman

William Morrow and Company, Inc.
New York 1981

Library of Congress Cataloging in Publication Data

Feldman, Daniel L
    Reforming government.

    "Morrow quill paperbacks."

    Bibliography: p.
    Includes index.
    1. Corruption (in politics)—United States.
2. Governmental investigations—United States.
I. Title.
[JK2249.F44 1981b]   353.009'94   80-24964
ISBN 0-688 03729-1
ISBN 0-688-00349-4 (pbk.)

Printed in the United States of America

First Morrow Quill Paperback Edition

1 2 3 4 5 6 7 8 9 10

BOOK DESIGN BY BERNARD SCHLEIFER

In honor of my father,
HENRY ASHER FELDMAN,
who gave me the strength,
and in memory of my mother,
RENNIE ROCK FELDMAN, *who gave me the spirit.*

Acknowledgments

THERE ARE AT LEAST four categories of benefactors to whom I am indebted for this book: the public officials who were courageous enough to spearhead our battles for reform; my colleagues in government and in the press whose alliance enabled us to win those battles; the confidential sources who were willing to step forward in the public interest; and my good friends whose editorial advice helped me translate experience into text.

The first category is a small one, and first and foremost is United States Representative Elizabeth Holtzman. Congresswoman Holtzman's courage and integrity should not be news to anyone who has followed national politics in the last decade. Her entry onto the national scene with her electoral victory over the "dean of the House," Emanuel Celler, in 1972; her successful lawsuit to stop the bombing in Cambodia for a brief period during the Vietnam War; her crucial role in the House Judiciary Committee impeachment proceedings in 1974 firmly established her place in history as one of the rare politicians of unquestioned commitment to conscience, coupled with extraordinary intellect and ability. This will seem excessively panegyric only to those who do not know her record well. For me, her sponsorship of the 1976 food program investigation launched me on the path that resulted in this book. My system of investigation and reform was born in the techniques that Congresswoman Holtzman and I applied in the exciting and seminal days of that battle.

7

If my system was born under Congresswoman Holtzman's sponsorship, it developed and grew to maturity during my association with Assemblyman Charles Schumer as chairman of the Assembly Subcommittee on City Management and later as chairman of the Committee on Legislative Oversight and Investigation. His decision to hire me as counsel and director gave me the platform I needed to practice and refine the work of investigation and reform. Schumer's own boundless confidence in our ability to fight and win, along with his intelligence and commitment, was among our best weapons.

My fellow soldiers in the trenches were several, and the moral support they provided over the years, as well as their practical assistance, made our work possible. In the beginning there were Ibby Lang, Gary Deane, and myself; with them I shared some of the best and most exciting of my investigations. Richard Meislin, Charles Kaiser, John Flannery, Steve Bauman, and Nick Pileggi worked closely with or in our inner circle and provided excellence when nothing less would have sufficed. The intelligence, talent, and good spirits of my esteemed friend, colleague, and former associate Josh Howard helped see me through some very difficult times. I hope I will be forgiven by the scores of other reporters and reformers not mentioned here whose support and assistance were critical at various times, but whose involvement with us was of shorter duration.

Many of the confidential sources who helped us must remain anonymous, and those I thank now; they know who they are and deserve to feel very proud of their contributions. For some the need for confidentiality has passed; Wendy Cooper, Gloria Lawrence, Dan Suster, Dennis Weiscopf, and Ira Hertzoff all played crucial roles at times when it was not easy for them to have done so.

This story would not have been told had it not been for those who helped me tell it. Eunice Riedel, my editor at William Morrow, has my permanent affection and admiration not only for deciding to publish the book, reason enough, but also for her invariably accurate observations of ways to make it better. I thank goodness for Arlene McKay, my chief sounding board, who kept me from meandering off into hopelessly speculative digressions, made sure there was at least some modicum of consistency in my logic and tone, and helped maintain a degree of liveliness in both the book and the author.

My good friend Regina Paul performed a labor of love in a massive fine-tooth editorial combing of several chapters, for which I shall be eternally grateful. Tappan King and Beth Meacham made me stop hiding my light under a bushel. Susan Schwartz was the first editor who said the book was worth publishing and helped give me the confidence to keep trying. Extremely valuable criticisms and suggestions on Chapters 2 and 3 came from Lotte Feinberg, Robert Horkovich, Susan Schwartz, and Susan Berkowitz; on Chapter 1, from Enid Stubin; on Chapters 7 through 18, from Arlene McKay; on Chapters 11 through 17, from Regina Paul and Jay Haas.

Contents

12 REFORMING GOVERNMENT

Introduction

THOUGH WASTE AND CORRUPTION have accompanied the growth of government in the past few decades in the United States, citizens still react more often with tired resignation rather than with fury to the latest evidence that government does not adequately police itself.

Even the powerful can find reform frustrating. Mayors or presidents who try to reform their own administrations find it, in FDR's words, like "punching a feather bed. You punch it with your left and you punch it with your right until you are finally exhausted, and then you find the damn bed just as it was before you started punching."

But there are methods for making government more efficient and more honest. This book is based on the successful use of a system of investigation and reform. The results, in numerous cases of mismanagement and corruption, were better, cleaner government practices.

I am presenting, therefore, a blueprint for government reform, based on exposure of abuse, designed to embarrass officials into doing right. This book reviews the many actors who can play the reformer role, sets forth the system's basic premises, and answers the following questions: How do investigations of government abuse start? What are the best techniques of investigative research? How do you apply pressure to produce meaningful change?

Those are questions I wanted to answer when I first went to work for Elizabeth Holtzman. In the years I worked for her and for the New York state legislature I found some answers that will be helpful to anyone interested in government reform.

My own interest in government, politics, and the public interest stretches back to when I was seven, when my parents sent me to street corners to distribute Adlai Stevenson-for-President campaign literature. Although neither of my parents was involved with government, both were deeply concerned with public issues, and my mother was politically active on a volunteer level. Our family also has a long tradition of not being particularly good at or interested in making money. It may have been inevitable that I would seek a career in public service.

My first opportunity came in my junior year at Columbia College in New York City, when I worked at a low-level job in New York City government. In my senior year I was a Sloan Foundation New York City Urban Fellow. This was a new fellowship program that allowed twenty students to work at a responsible level of city government in Mayor John V. Lindsay's administration, which in 1969 still seemed something of a second Camelot, particularly to the student community.

Among the most impressive people I came to know there was Elizabeth Holtzman, then assistant to Mayor Lindsay for parks. At the end of my fellowship year, I worked in her successful race for local office in Brooklyn. Two years later, after my second year at Harvard Law School, I assisted her again, this time in her successful campaign for Congress. In my third year at Harvard, I first tested murky political waters for myself and commuted to New York City to run for City Council. I lost with 35 percent of the vote. Practicing law for the next year, I saved some money and spent it on my second try, which I lost with 40 percent of the vote.

I then went back to work for Holtzman, this time as paid staff, when she asked me to run her district congressional office in Brooklyn. Among many other activities, I supervised four caseworkers who dealt with citizens seeking our help in solving problems with government agencies—late Social Security checks; uncollected garbage; city housing offices that failed to help get heat and hot water from landlords. Also, in the congresswoman's absence, I handled community-group problems with government agencies. Such neighborhood issues involved obtaining federal funds for repaving a parkway and debating the mayor to keep him from closing one of our local police precinct houses. I also had to make sure that the press was informed of our doings and that the congresswoman's visits were rationally planned, and I attended to the innumerable details that kept the office functioning smoothly.

In July 1976 my job suddenly changed into that of a full-time investigator of a federal food program, and that is where this book begins. There was no institutional, legal, or traditional basis for this transformation. Classically the United States political tradition stresses the balance of power among the legislative, executive, and judicial branches of government. Congress, as the funding source for programs operated by the executive branch, has monitoring functions. But those functions are usually relegated to appropriate committees or subcommittees. For the food program investigation, the appropriate subcommittee was the Health, Education, and Welfare Subcommittee of the Ways and Means Committee. Generally these subcommittees are not equipped for in-depth field investigation. Committee members usually just review budgets and question witnesses in Washington. In this particular case an additional obstacle was that the chairman of the subcommittee had a special interest in *not* investigating the program in question.

The other traditional monitoring tool of Congress is the General Accounting Office, which performs inquiries at the behest of members of Congress. The GAO is thorough, professional, and competent, but it is slow, is too small to monitor a nation full of programs, and lacks the political drive to seek headlines that will generate pressure on executive branch agencies. The GAO is modeled on the British system, in which the government auditor is responsible for certifying before Parliament that the public treasury has not been misspent. But neither the British nor other European nations have a balance of powers among branches of government quite comparable to ours. The American system alone is designed to police itself. Still less is there a foreign parallel with the institutional context that enabled me to do investigative work. Equivalent roles are possible, however, in the rest of the world. Although

the American governmental and political systems are especially well suited to my kind of work, similar investigations
can be done anywhere there is a free press.

Thus, although the role I assumed in Holtzman's Brooklyn
office was not quite traditional, the job did fill a vacuum in
the modern American governmental system. For, with the
enormous growth of the executive branch in the past several
decades, congressional countervailing forces must be strength-
ened. Well established subject-area congressional committees
and subcommittees may just be too cozy with the bureaucracies they are supposed to monitor. And, unlike the GAO, individual members of Congress and their district staffs have
much to gain and can enhance their careers with favorable
publicity. One effective way to generate publicity is by con-
ducting successful investigations. The district offices are well
suited for the investigations of executive branch programs because daily they hear complaints about how the government is
not working properly.

In 1977 I left Holtzman's staff for a new job where I had
the opportunity to assume a role a step, but only a step, closer
to the traditional legislative function—this time at the state
level. Because of my successful work on the food program,
I was asked to become counsel to a new subcommittee of the
New York State Assembly, the lower house of the state legislature. Although state subcommittees do sometimes exercise
watchdog powers over programs in the areas of their jurisdiction, this subcommittee was unusual in being a state institution created to oversee municipal affairs. Called the
Subcommittee on City Management, it had no precisely de-
fined goals. The chairman, New York State Assemblyman
Charles Schumer, a legislator from Brooklyn, New York, and I
interpreted our work as looking into anything to do with city
government—a broad terrain. With a budget of more than
$13.5 billion a year, New York City's government is larger
than all but a few of the fifty states.

Also unusual was that I was stationed not at the Capitol in
Albany, but in New York City. I never went near the legislative process in Albany. This was because my job was to
perform investigations in the field. I started with a cubbyhole
office, a part-time researcher, and a total annual budget of

$20,000 that had to pay my salary plus all expenses the office incurred. Later I had a full-time assistant and summer help from one or two students. Despite rather modest staff and funding, we uncovered and investigated a wide range of city corruption from drug-abuse treatment centers and port issues to parking tickets and real estate.

The difference between my work for Holtzman and my subsequent work for the Subcommittee on City Management reflected an increasing awareness of the need to police government growth. For Holtzman I was a self-styled investigator able to serve only because of the particular interests of one member of Congress. When I joined the subcommittee, however, the New York state legislature—a governmental body—sanctioned its activities, at least in principle. Our type of investigation no longer depended entirely on the whim of an individual legislator.

The state legislature's appreciation of the need for our style of work grew with our successes. In 1979, in recognition of our progress, the speaker of the Assembly promoted the subcommittee to a full committee. Its purpose was spelled out by law, and its title was explicit: the Committee on Legislative Oversight and Investigation. Assemblyman Charles Schumer was again chairman.

A vague precedent existed for our committee. Previously the speaker's office had included an Office of Legislative Oversight and Analysis, headed by a former reporter. But the speaker has many avenues of power, and although that office was able to issue numerous excellent reports on major government problems, its role was limited.

Our committee had the advantage of being a separate standing entity rather than merely a part of the speaker's office. Moreover, with an assemblyman as chairman, we were harnessing the political ambition of a young legislator to the cause of investigation and reform. Unlike the speaker, this young committee chairman had far more incentive to use his committee to go for the headlines which can expedite reform.

With the full committee status, I had grander quarters and a staff of four, sometimes five, full-time employees. In addition to continuing work on some of the previous scandals, we investigated subjects as diverse as overhauling the thoroughbred racing industry, vermin in the public schools, lack of mechanics to repair fire department trucks, overcharging by school bus operators, and streamlining jury selection.

Subsequent chapters will illustrate the application of our system in a dozen well-publicized examples of my own investigations. These are the stories behind the news, told from a perspective that reveals what came before the press coverage and what came after. They demonstrate that meaningful reform is possible, that good government can be good politics, and that a system designed to accomplish these goals on the city, state, or federal levels is ready and waiting.

This newly burgeoning monitoring role of the legislative branch is a valuable addition to its power over the possible excesses of a busy and powerful executive branch.

REFORMING

GOVERNMENT

1

Sandwiches in the Streets

SIXTEEN-THOUSAND SANDWICHES were sitting in an empty lot on Bay Street in Bensonhurst, a middle-class neighborhood in Brooklyn that lies about eight miles south of Manhattan's southern tip. Tuna fish, bologna, and peanut butter was baking in the hot July sun.

That summer—1976—wasted food was not a rare sight in Bensonhurst. Nor was it rare in poor sections of New York City, such as East New York and Brownsville. The question was why food was going to waste in neighborhoods where so many people were living on welfare. As it turned out, of course, the food in the streets that summer did not come from the cupboards of the poor. The food came from a federally funded lunch program under the auspices of the United States Department of Agriculture.

Throughout the school year federal tax dollars subsidize free lunches that are eaten by millions of schoolchildren. To ensure that the poorest of these children eat balanced meals when school is out, the federal government in 1968 enacted a $32 million nationwide summertime lunch program. By 1976 the program had expanded to more than $120 million nationwide.

These dollars bought the 16,000 sandwiches dumped in Bensonhurst and other food that was spoiled and pilfered at sites where social service organizations were supposed to be feeding children. And those dollars bought the carton of milk thrown at Democratic Congresswoman Elizabeth Holtzman when she came to visit one of the lunch distribution sites that summer.

By September 1976, though, investigations by Holtzman and her staff had resulted in the cancellation of contracts with many of the social service groups entrusted with distributing the food, and later the officials charged with administering the summertime lunch program in New York would be fired.

Two months of probing by two members of Holtzman's staff, who were occasionally assisted by others in her ten-person local district office, led down a trail which went around the country, down the halls of Congress, and into the offices of high-level federal officials, including Gerald R. Ford, President of the United States.

I was Holtzman's executive assistant that summer. I ran her congressional district office in Brooklyn and represented her at local meetings when she was in Washington. Once the sandwiches were found, I also took up the investigation of the food in the streets.

Soon after school had let out and the summer lunch program was under way, we began to get complaints from citizens about food being dumped at various summertime lunch program sites. We had received a few such complaints the previous summer, but when Holtzman had asked the Department of Agriculture for an explanation, it had replied that everything concerning the summer food program was under investigation and it therefore could not supply us with any information. Now, with fresh complaints a year later, we decided to check out the situation on our own. During the week of July 11, 1976, several of us from Holtzman's office visited a number of sites where we saw for ourselves the containers of soured milk, rotting oranges, and other spoiled food strewn about the sidewalks. We returned to the office and looked up the federal regulations that told us how the program was really supposed to run. Holtzman decided to make a surprise visit to two of the sites. And to make sure our message stuck, we invited along the press, an official from the Department of Agriculture, which was responsible for the lunch program, and two auditors from the General Accounting Office, which monitors expenditures by federal departments.

Tom Raftery, covering the story for the New York *Daily News*, wrote: "Ms. Holtzman met children lugging away shopping bags full of food, edibles supposed to be consumed at the distribution site. They readily admitted that they were taking home milk, sandwiches, oranges and doughnuts for their parents and other adults, she said." Farther down in Raftery's story appeared the information that although this particular site had received 1,150 lunches, the site supervisor had said first that it had received only 350 lunches, the "normal" amount it was listed for.

By the time Raftery's story appeared on Monday morning Holtzman's office was flooded with telephone complaints from every part of the city about the program. Channel 4, whose reporter had gone on the tour, had already played the story Friday night. Once news editors saw the juicy coverage of children and adults carrying away bags of lunches and throwing food all over the street, all the press wanted the story. Thursday's New York *Post* featured a photograph of its reporter carrying a case of milk he had been given free at a food site. *The New York Times* began its coverage of the story on July 22.

In New York City 600,000 children, or 41 percent of the school population, received school lunches. However, under federal regulations, the summer food program could provide lunch to any child who came to a site in an area in which at least a third of the children were eligible for school lunch program meals.

Thus, 1.4 million summer lunches per day were approved for distribution in New York City's 1976 summer food program. Therefore, 58 percent of the entire population of the city under the age of nineteen should have been receiving lunch. This, of course, was not the case. The Community Council of Greater New York later estimated that about 600,000 children actually did receive food, but that much of this was inedible. The remaining 800,000 lunches a day, paid for by taxpayers, were not going to children. As Holtzman was to testify in Washington on July 22, 1976, some of this food was being thrown at neighbors. Some of it was picked up at the distribution sites by children who then sold it elsewhere in the neighborhood. Adults were carrying off some of it by the shopping cart load. And a few police officers were even taking the food home to feed their pets.

But by then we were already moving to a higher level of malfeasance. We were tracing the federal monies through the state level, where the program was handled by the State Education Department, to the local groups that were wasting it. The U.S. Department of Agriculture based its funding of each state's share of the program on the number of needy children in the state. The state entered into contracts with sponsors: non-profit institutions that undertook to distribute food to children at locations under their supervision. Before the program began, most sponsors advertised for food vendors, asking vendors to compete against each other for contracts. Any sponsor directing a program for which reimbursement was to exceed $10,000 was required to select vendors through open, public, competitive bidding.

This competitive process was designed to protect the children, by assuring that they got the best possible food, and the taxpayer, by assuring the lowest cost per meal.

Reimbursement to the vendor was based on the number of meals supplied: a maximum of 80.75 cents per lunch and lesser amounts for other meals. Reimbursement to the sponsor for the sponsor's administrative costs was also based on the number of meals supplied: 6.5 cents per lunch and less for other meals. Reimbursement to the state agency was also based on volume of meals supplied: 2 percent of the state program's cost. With about 1.4 million lunches a day approved for New York City by the State Education Department in 1976, this represented sizable amounts of money for everyone involved, and everyone involved had an incentive to inflate the numbers.

When Holtzman testified on July 22, she was holding a site application approved by the State Education Department. The application was for a food site serving more than 1,000 meals a day:

> The application describes the site as a school. It is not. The application states that indoor space is available; in fact, there is none. The application states that refrigerators exist for food storage. There are no such refrigerators. Yet, this site was approved. . . .

She pointed out that since the site had to be inspected before it could be approved, a "statement of inspection" *had* been filled out, but the rest of the inspection form was blank.

Every day we sent lists of site complaints to Dr. Stanley Campbell, the director of the program for the State Education Department's New York City operations. He did not seem to be aware of the abuses we uncovered, that his own inspectors were approving highly unsatisfactory sites, or even of how many food distribution sites there actually were. Since Campbell's superiors in Albany were sophisticated and politically savvy, it is not unreasonable to consider the possibility that he was selected intentionally, under the assumption that all sorts of shenanigans could go on under his nose and he'd never notice them.

By this time defenders of the program were ready with a salvo of press events of their own. One congressman, who toured a summer food program site which appeared to be operating well, concluded that despite a few "rotten apples" in the barrel, the problems were not endemic. However, we later learned that this congressman had given advance notice of his visit to the site. The program sponsor, who was no better than the others, had thus had time to correct violations.

A tour of another site, the Rose of Sharon Church in Bedford-Stuyvesant, was conducted by Richard Habersham-Bey, who would later be convicted of misusing poverty program funds. Habersham-Bey was an officer of one of the summer food program sponsors, Bedford-Stuyvesant Youth-In-Action. Charges by Habersham-Bey's group, reported under an August 7, 1976, headline in *The New York Times* reading "Child Lunch Site Closings Held Biased," were that program sites were being closed for technical reasons because 1976 "is the first year that there's any appreciable amount of black people involved."

On August 12 the theme of Holtzman as racist was repeated by what purported to be a newly formed citywide parents' group called United Parents to Feed All Children. They picketed Holtzman's office with signs reading "Miss Holtzman, are you poor with children to feed?," "Holtzman, guess who's coming to dinner?," and "Holtzman, I need food to grow." The *Daily News* account of the incident noted that some of the parents had said that they came from the East Harlem Community Corporation and Acción Cívica Evangélica, two sponsors in the program. When I questioned the group leader about the picketers' admission that they were associated with program sponsors, she said, "They shouldn't have told you that!" When I asked whether her members were not permitted to speak freely, she said, "Well, you shouldn't have asked them that!"

But this embarrassment did not deter supporters of the program. The following week another protest outside Holtzman's office was led by a black would-be politician whose press release said, among other things, "We are certain that these attacks [on the food program] are borne out of [Holtzman's] need to perpetuate the terrible poverty that exists in minority communities by denying its children food and its adults a brief but much-needed period of employment during the summer months." We were later told that white vendors in the food program had drafted this press release with considerable merriment, replete with scathing comments about the literacy of the blacks for whom they were preparing the release. These incidents show how terms like "racist" and accusations of insensitivity to the needs of the poor can be used.

But our focus was narrowing toward the center of the program's corruption. At the end of July we began to review the contract bidding files at the State Education Department. This agency's "contract specialist" was an unsung heroine of the investigation. Ironically the circumstances of her employment illustrated some of the abuses of the program.

As mentioned above, Dr. Stanley Campbell was in charge of the State Education Department's operations in New York City. The city portion constituted more than 90 percent of the entire summer food program in the state. The statewide director was Dr. Thomas Calvin, who supervised Dr. Campbell from Albany. At a preliminary meeting before the program got under way, Calvin recommended that Campbell employ Wendy Cooper, who had just finished her first year of law school and needed a summer job. Campbell argued that he had applications from students who, having finished their second year of law school, should be considered over Wendy. Calvin prevailed, and Wendy got the job of enforcing compliance with contractual bidding requirements in New York City's $80 million summer food program.

By the first week in July—six weeks after she had started work—Wendy had taught herself enough about the regulations governing the program to ask the sponsors for copies of basic documents: the advertisements they had taken out as evidence that they had made a public announcement of bidding for their contracts; and their eventual reasons for choosing the vendors they chose, including information about who the lowest bidder was and, if the lowest bidder had not been chosen, an explanation of why he had not.

Thus, when I came to look at the contract documents, Campbell sent me to Wendy Cooper. Probably unknown to Campbell, and certainly unknown to Calvin, Wendy had fairly good files by then indicating the shortcomings of each contract. I arrived expecting to be met by a hostile and defensive bureaucrat. Instead, Wendy Cooper, who had been living with the frustration inevitable in an honest and able person faced with a scandalously mismanaged government organization, tried to make sure that I did not overlook any of the contractual violations she herself had found.

On August 10 the *Daily News'* headline read "Holtzman Hints at Lunch Contract Collusion." The *Times*, ever more cautious, said only, "Food Program Contracts Questioned." What we found, in essence, was that contracts between sponsors and vendors for delivery of food had been signed, in two key instances, the day *before* bids for the contracts were to have been opened. Holtzman said, "If the date for the public opening of bids was after the date the contract was signed, any such public opening was no more than a charade. No real competition for the contract can have taken place."

One of the contracts in question was for the B'nai Torah Institute. The *Times* quoted a representative's response that the dating "had to be a clerical error." The other predated contract belonged to the Hassidic Corporation for Urban Concerns. Not for a year would the State Education Department act on this latter contract. In June 1977 the department finally decided that the predating had been no mere clerical error and therefore denied the Hassidic Corporation for Urban Concerns the right to participate in the 1977 program:

The time sequence made a mockery out of applicable

bid requirements, indicating, at best, that applicant prematurely opened and reviewed the bids which had been submitted, or that in the absence of such preview, applicant collusively determined to enter into a contract with a predetermined food vendor without regard to the results of the formal bid opening on June 22, 1976. [June 30, 1977 decision denying participation]

It was only chance, perhaps, that brought special attention to B'nai Torah and the Hassidic Corporation for Urban Concerns at this time. On August 10 they were still just two of the twenty contracts in violation of one rule or another, out of thirty we had reviewed. We did not know at that time that these were the flagship sponsors of two nationwide organizations, the two that would prove to have been the most successful in extracting money from the summer food program.

Other contracts were not preceded by advertisements providing adequate information about the date, time, or place of the bid opening. Some left out information about the bids and relative costs of competing vendors. And only 10 of the 134 contracts were signed at prices below the *maximum* price the federal government permitted for the lunches, raising obvious questions about whether anyone had bid for those contracts below the maximum level. Later we were to show that at least 80 of the contracts were made in violation of the competitive bidding requirements.

Commenting on the predated contracts and on the 16,000 sandwiches found dumped in Bensonhurst, the *Post* editorial of August 10 asked:

Why? For whose profit? To keep what numbers up, falsify what distribution records? Is there a connection between this fantastic episode and the latest disclosure by Rep. Holtzman that two "nonprofit" organizations acting as sponsors of the Summer Food Program have signed multimillion dollar contracts with private food companies before the opening of bids in an apparently collusive operation?

Meanwhile, our efforts were bearing their first fruit. The blitz inspection of records ordered by the Department of Agriculture after Holtzman's initial allegations resulted in an $8.5 million cut in allocations, based on evidence of the actual needs of children served by the sponsors. The cut was announced by Dr. Thomas Calvin on August 11, the day after the Holtzman press conference on contract violations. While the timing may have been coincidental, Calvin was certainly an experienced enough bureaucrat to know when his department could sorely use an appearance of activism and toughness.

At the same time that I was analyzing the contract bidding documents, another Holtzman aide was analyzing complaints by sponsors' employees that they had never been paid. This aide also investigated hygiene—or its lack—at vendor plants and other site complaints.

We prepared to issue a massive site violation report on August 13, including falsifications in applications and inflated meal counts in thirty-one of the thirty-eight sample sites reviewed. We found state approvals for a site at a nonexistent address, multiple sponsors at one site (all receiving federal reimbursement), sites authorized and reimbursed for the feeding of 500 children when no more than 20 could possibly have fitted into the premises. Our report was furnished to the State Education Department, but we never released it. We were getting away from the site violations, the newscasts of black children carrying shopping bags of lunches away from sites. We were past accusations of being antiblack and were now being accused of anti-Semitism.

The pattern of vendor selections by the B'nai Torah organization was striking. B'nai Torah consisted of five individual sponsors in the B'nai Torah umbrella organization: the B'nai Torah Institute; Bais Isaac Zvi; Special Programs for Americans; Nutrition for Youth; and the Queens Assistance Program. Although they were only five out of forty-nine sponsors, together they accounted for about 10 percent of the city's summer food program budget.

With respect to four of the sponsors, only four vendors bid for their contracts: Food Service Dynamics; JABCO; Hi-Score; and Meals & Snacks. Each vendor bid the same amount, the most the federal government would reimburse: 81 cents per lunch. Each of the four got at least one contract from the B'nai Torah group. Each sponsor gave reasons for selecting the vendors it chose, but when the sponsors are a single entity, such reasons are dubious at best. As Holtzman's press release stated:

> . . . sponsor B'nai Torah Institute chose the vendor JABCO, saying it could provide "efficient and satisfactory attention and prompt personal service." On the other hand, Bais Isaac Zvi rejected JABCO, saying it was "not convinced of their experience in food service and of their financial capabilities."

Similarly, sponsor Special Programs for Americans chose vendor Meals & Snacks, saying that Meals & Snacks had "performed reasonably well" the previous year. But curiously, sponsor Nutrition for Youth rejected Meals & Snacks, saying that its deliveries the previous year had often been late.

I needed proof that all five groups were really the same entity. As all were supposedly nonprofit organizations (the only real requirement for participation in the New York summer food program), this was no problem. The Internal Revenue Service must make available to the public documents upon which tax-exempt status has been granted to any organization. These IRS documents, listing the organizations' officers, showed that Victor Mayer and either Sidney, Lieb, Abraham, or Pinchus Pinter were the top executives of each sponsor in the group. Wendy Cooper's memoranda had said that basic similarities in the group's documents submitted to the State Education Department "strongly indicated that these are not five separate organizations but only one sponsor, B'nai Torah." B'nai Torah's contention all along was that the five groups were affiliated—they all were listed on the same letterhead. But they persisted in maintaining that management decisions for the five were made independently of each other.

At first I was puzzled because the fifth B'nai Torah, or "Pinter," sponsor, the Queens Assistance Program, had one of the very few contracts in the entire food program signed at a price below the maximum reimbursable level, although only fractionally lower. The explanation? *Only* in the case of the Queens Assistance Program did an outside vendor, not one of the four who bid for and received all the other contracts, bid. This outside bidder, not part of the cabal, had unexpectedly introduced competition with a low bid. The cabal had to offer an even lower bid to win the contract because the Pinter group would otherwise have had to explain why it had rejected the lowest bid in its records.

Even more enlightening, the winner of the Queens Assistance Program contract, Food Service Dynamics, bid the usual maximum for Bais Isaac Zvi's contract two days later—and won it. Holtzman asked, "How can the Pinter group justify accepting the highest possible price from a vendor which had previously bid at a lower price?" Moreover, it had paid the highest price for the larger contract and the lower price for the smaller contract—completely reversing economic principles. As it turned out, the culinary offerings of Food Service Dynamics were among the most interesting of the summer and broke Jewish dietary laws that forbid mixing meat with dairy products, laws that Jewish community groups might have been expected to safeguard. The menu included "kosher" cheeseburgers made from moldy meat—a unique taste treat that Holtzman dubbed the "open-faced frozen knish sandwich"—moldy chicken, and "kosher" salami and cheese sandwiches.

The circumstantial case of collusion between the Pinter sponsors and vendors was overwhelming. We went back to the 1975 records and found that the five Pinter sponsors that year had awarded contracts exclusively to Meals & Snacks, Hi-Score, and "Luigi Goldstein Inc." Barry Goldstein, a partner in Luigi Goldstein Inc., was the general manager of Food Service Dynamics in 1976. Luigi Goldstein in 1976 held the lease for the second floor of 47-05 Metropolitan Avenue in Brooklyn, the space that housed Food Service Dynamics and JABCO. As Holtzman said:

> If Luigi Goldstein is the parent of Food Service Dynamics and JABCO, then in essence the same vendors were selected this year and last year. The statistical likelihood that this was the result of free market forces and competitive bidding is virtually zero.

The most fertile item in the charges leveled against B'nai

Torah proved to be our disclosure that a canceled $500 check in State Education Department files written by Meals & Snacks to Special Programs for Americans was dated May 27, 1976, thus establishing, we thought, some kind of financial relationship between the two. This relationship, between a vendor, who was supposed to respond to competitive bidding at arm's length, and the sponsor, who offered a contract, would therefore have been established more than two weeks before invitations to bid were even sent out. Later Holtzman noticed that the address listed for Meals & Snacks on the check was 50 West Twenty-third Street in Manhattan, one of the main headquarters for the B'nai Torah organization. The superintendent said that there had been no Meals & Snacks as occupant in his seven years with the building. When Eric Fettmann, the reporter who had covered the story for the New York *Post*, asked B'nai Torah's Victor Mayer about the date of the Meals & Snacks check, Mayer explained that the check was not for the New York program at all, but for the Philadelphia branch of Special Programs for Americans. Until that comment we did not realize that we were dealing with a national organization. We began to make liberal use of the Federal Telecommunications Service, the long-distance telephone service available to congressional offices.

We tracked down the administrators of the summer food program in various states. We asked those administrators for the names of the sponsors or vendors contracted to distribute the food. When direct questioning or cajoling failed to induce vendors to tell us about their operations or ownership, we reminded them that a member of Congress could subpoena them to testify under oath. That usually convinced the person on the other end of the telephone to answer our questions.

We found Pinter organizations in St. Louis, Chicago, Philadelphia, and New Jersey. In St. Louis the sponsor was listed under the auspices of the highly reputable Rabbinical College of St. Louis. But the Midwest Regional Office of the Department of Agriculture told me that telephone calls seeking early payments on behalf of its program came from a Yitzchok Scholnick, whom we had already identified as the vice-president of Bais Isaac Zvi, a Pinter sponsor in Brooklyn. Rabbi

Lieb Pinter, the overall head of the organization, himself called Agriculture twice on its behalf.

And which sponsor emerged victorious from the competitive bidding process conducted in St. Louis to win the food contract for this program? None other than Hi-Score of St. Louis, incorporated in Missouri by the same George Ribowsky who owned the New York Hi-Score.

In Chicago, Special Programs for Americans signed a $1.6 million contract with Nutritional Foods, Inc. We were puzzled. Where were our vendor friends from New York? A hunch—was Nutritional Foods ever known by any other name? It was: Hi-Score Foods of Chicago. Some verbal browbeating of employees produced the name of its sole stockholder, George Ribowsky.

In New Jersey, Special Programs for Americans' $2.8 million contract was signed with Food Distributors of America. By now the pattern was clear enough; routine inquiries determined that Food Distributors of America happened to share an office with a company called Hi-Score.

In Philadelphia, St. Louis, Chicago, and New York, B'nai Torah had required as a condition of bidding for its contracts an interest-free loan from the vendor, with no return date of payment specified. No other sponsor anywhere ever included such a requirement. Most businessmen would call such an arrangement (written into the contract by B'nai Torah) a bribe. In Chicago the State Education Department told me that it was suspicious of this provision and checked with the Department of Agriculture's legal division, which told them it was fine. In New York, characteristically, Dr. Campbell's assistant director told me that his office never realized the provision was in the contract at all until I had asked about it. In New Jersey a gutsy State Education Department summer food program administrator named Carol Steinberger threw B'nai Torah representatives out of her office, and they came back with a new contract without that provision. In all, B'nai Torah had well over $12 million worth of contracts in the 1976 summer food program.

In the course of our national investigation of the Pinter organization, we heard allegations that Pinter had political

connections at the highest levels of government. An anonymous letter came in:

> Pinter, who is a leading figure in the food program, is
> a personal friend of Ford. When Ford was senator and
> Vice President, Pinter spoke to him regularly. At a dinner
> honoring B'nai Torah, the front for Pinter's fraud, Ford
> was the guest speaker and referred to Pinter as "my good
> friend Lieb." Ford was Vice President then.
>
> Ribowsky, a leading vendor, was a neighbor of Pinter
> and was a salaried worker for him. They are close friends.
> Ribowsky was previously a poor carpet salesman. Pinter
> set Ribowsky up in the vending business and is a secret
> partner with him.
>
> I wish you luck in your investigation. I don't think
> much will come of it, however, because Pinter knows and
> pays off lots of people, including some elected officials.
>
> I cannot sign my name because I know better. He's a
> real crook. As one congressman told me after meeting with
> Pinter—"There goes the biggest crook in Washington."
> That's quite an accomplishment.

Anonymous letters were not the sort of documentation upon
which we could base charges, although food distribution site
complaints which had been telephoned into our office, usually
anonymously, were borne out, even by State Education Department reviews, in more than 90 percent of the cases. But
additional accusations along these lines were surfacing.

Chicago summer food program officials had reported to us
that Rabbi Pinter had showed them pictures of himself with
President Ford and Secretary of Agriculture Earl Butz as
demonstrations of the Rabbi's credibility at the highest levels
of government. In New York, Eric Fettmann of the *Post*, Richard Meislin of the *Times*, and Tom Collins of the *Daily News*,
three excellent reporters who had been assigned to Holtzman's
investigations by their respective newspapers, all told us of

unsubstantiated but numerous and plausible accounts of Pinter's high-level political connections.

In September I spoke before the American Jewish Committee Executive Board in New York City on the summer food program and the problems inherent in dealing with sharp operators who made unscrupulous use of the title "rabbi" and who, in so doing, hurt the image of the Jewish community. One member in attendance said that she thought her friend in Miami, who worked for the American Jewish Committee there, might have some information of interest to us on Pinter.

In late September I received a fascinating set of documents from Miami, including a letter stating, "In addition to the brochure, we have picked out a selected set of pictures and correspondence which are indicative of the support that B'nai Torah has enjoyed in official circles." There was a letter from Secretary of Agriculture Earl Butz to Rabbi Lieb Pinter stating, "How can I ever express my appreciation to you and your associates for the lovely tribute you extended to me last Sunday evening when you presented the Humanitarian Award of the B'nai Torah Institute." Another item was a brief thank-you note from Vice President Gerald Ford. Where the secretary had typed "Dear Rabbi Pinter," "Rabbi Pinter" had been crossed out, and "Lieb" had been written in. Then there was a letter from President Gerald Ford, remembering "with great pleasure my participation in your last dinner," praising B'nai Torah's efforts in "preparing America's young people for leadership and responsibility in the future," and concluding "with warmest personal regards." A series of photographs of Pinter at the White House with Ford and with seven members of Congress, including Daniel Flood, graphically illustrated the nature of Pinter's influence.

Since the summer food program was run under the auspices of the Department of Agriculture, either Earl Butz did have some idea of the nature of B'nai Torah's involvement in the program, or he was soaringly ignorant about his department. When we had wanted information in 1975, Agriculture had told us that the program was "under investigation." And Agriculture told the Chicago State Education Department that

Pinter's "interest-free loan" provision did not violate the competitive bidding rules.

Certain charges, however, were more specific. In a memorandum to Holtzman on August 3, 1976, another aide and I asked, "Who is Pinter's man in Flood's office?" The answer would be front-page news a year and a half later, when federal prosecutors disclosed that Stephen Elko, a former aide to Flood, had told them that Lieb Pinter had paid Elko $3,000 and Flood $7,000 to intervene on Pinter's behalf in connection with federal job training grants Pinter wanted. Flood, since 1968, had chaired the House Appropriations Subcommittee on Labor, Health, Education, and Welfare, which has jurisdiction over food program and job program appropriations.

On Friday, May 11, 1978, Pinter pleaded guilty in federal court to bribing Congressman Flood for his intervention with federal agencies. Pinter could have been sentenced to up to fifteen years, but in recognition of the evidence he provided against Flood, he was actually sentenced on June 22, 1978, to two years in prison and a $17,000 fine.

In 1976 B'nai Torah was planning its annual dinner for December of that year. This time the New York City mayor was to have received the Humanitarian Award, and Representative Morris Udall was to have been the guest speaker. But Richard Meislin, the *Times* reporter covering the program, called the mayor's press secretary to ask if he knew what kind of organization was honoring the mayor. When Meislin told him, the press secretary said something along the lines of "Oh, my God," and the mayor promptly canceled his appearance. The mayor had an election year ahead of him. Udall canceled after learning of the mayor's cancellation.

But B'nai Torah was not the sum of what was wrong in the summer food program. B'nai Torah was only one of four major influence groups we uncovered. Also revealed as exploiters were Bedford-Stuyvesant Youth-In-Action, a Bronx-based group we came to call the Velez Empire because it was linked to City Councilman Ramon Velez, and the Crown Heights Community Corporation—all to be mentioned in subsequent chapters. So there was much more to do.

Despite Wendy Cooper's recommendation that advance payments for August be held up until compliance with bidding requirements had been determined, Calvin and Campbell gave out about $10 million in such payments in early August to sponsors whose contracts showed evidence of such problems. On September 10 Holtzman rounded up two other New York representatives—one black and one Puerto Rican—and they wrote a joint letter to Secretary Butz requesting that Agriculture remove from the State Education Department the power to disburse the balance of payments to sponsors. They suggested that Agriculture make such payments itself after determining who deserved what. With the Department of Agriculture under intense scrutiny, it would perform honestly. The State Education Department, even under scrutiny, seemed incapable of even rudimentary good sense or competence. On September 23 Agriculture wired the State Education Department prohibiting it from making any more payments, pending review by Agriculture. The signatures of the black and Puerto Rican representatives on the letter protected Holtzman from the usual protest of racism when the decision became public. But the next day's *Times* quoted an angry Calvin, who blamed "political pressure" for the cutoff of funds.

In December 1976 Holtzman called for the removal of Calvin and Campbell, citing their performance record. Campbell was removed in January 1977 and was replaced in February with Carol Steinberger, the courageous New Jersey administrator who had turned down the B'nai Torah interest-free loan requirement. Calvin's removal from the program was announced in February, but he continued to play a behind-the-scenes role in 1977. Apparently he engineered delays in the 1977 program, according to my sources in the State Education Department at that time, in an attempt to undercut Steinberger and thus indirectly discredit Holtzman's reforms.

In December Holtzman presented to the State Education Department and to the Department of Agriculture a detailed series of recommendations for reforming the administration of the program, including stringent requirements for sponsor approval and bidding. In early March the Department of Agriculture announced the official 1977 regulations, adopting most of Holtzman's suggestions.

The 1977 program was far from perfect. Steinberger's efforts were undercut by furious politicians, bureaucrats, and "community leaders" of the kind that had profited greatly from the 1976 program. But the contrast with 1976 was remarkable. The *Times*, in a September 3, 1977, headline, said, "City Food Program Is Losing Notoriety; It Ends a Season Relatively Free of Any Charges of Impropriety." The best description of the change was Murray Kempton's, this time in the *Post* of July 12, 1977:

> Rep. Elizabeth Holtzman of Brooklyn set forth yesterday to inspect the fruits of her lonely effort last summer to infuse the minimal decencies into the [summer] lunch program. . . .
>
> It is impossible to imagine that, without Elizabeth Holtzman, the summer lunch program would not have been as bad today as it was a year ago. The case of the B'nai Torah Institute is suggestive enough of the otherwise extraordinary official tolerance open to the undeserving greedy. . . .
>
> Queens Assistance's conduct of its 1975 [program] resulted in widespread enough protests of food spoilage to induce the District Attorney to subpoena its records.
>
> All the same, the State Education Department approved B'nai Torah as a sponsor for its 1975 summer lunch program with the unique disclaimer that, since the District Attorney had taken all its records into custody, there was no fair way to judge its prior performance. . . .
>
> Miss Holtzman persisted in her reproaches throughout last summer and the uniform official response was contempt.
>
> Secretary of Agriculture Butz replied to her protests by describing the summer lunch program as a Congressional aberration and implying that, for all of him, it could wallow in the obloquy it deserved.
>
> The State Education Department complained that its manful efforts to curb abuses in the program were being damaged by the interference of Congressmen and their staffs.
>
> But in the end, Rep. Holtzman won. The Dept. of Agriculture has tightened the summer lunch program's

rules; and the State Dept. of Education, without apology, has changed its manager.

In 1978 the State Education Department left the program entirely, claiming that the Department of Agriculture refused to give it enough money to administer the program properly. Once again Agriculture took over the local administration of the program, as it had in 1974 and 1975. As in those years, Agriculture's performance appeared to be slipshod. But this time Holtzman was watching, and when she threatened to criticize the program again, Agriculture—perhaps remembering Stanley Campbell's fate—jumped. The *Times*, on Tuesday, June 27, 1978, reported that the Department of Agriculture had withdrawn its approval of a Pinter-connected vendor, Food Service Dynamics, mere hours after Holtzman charged that it was being permitted to bid again. Holtzman explained Agriculture's seemingly instantaneous response: "On Friday, I learned that after my intention to publicize the vendor approved list was made known, Agriculture Department officials were literally scurrying to remove some of the worst vendors from the program."

Furthermore, after Holtzman criticized the federal administrator of the program, Agriculture again brought in Carol Steinberger to run it. The federal department made these changes late, once again hamstringing Steinberger's efforts to run a good program. Undoubtedly some new exploiters will have filled the shoes of the old ones. But it was inconceivable that even under the worst of circumstances a rerun of 1976 would be permitted.

Pinter went to prison. The proprietors of Food Service Dynamics were indicted in November 1979. Two city councilmen (one of them Ramon Velez) who had been involved in the scandal were out of office. Flood resigned from Congress in disgrace on January 31, 1980, and pleaded guilty to conspiracy to accept bribes. The Crown Heights Community Corporation and Bedford-Stuyvesant Youth-In-Action lost their antipoverty contracts with the city.

Sometimes reform works.

2

Who Are the Reformers?

ONE REASON GOVERNMENT HAS too much power is that citizens abdicate theirs. Any citizen of the United States can adopt at least some of the tools of reform to fight against government abuse. Fortunately some do.

Robert Lowry, for example, a Maryland painter who wasn't getting federal contracts no matter how low he bid, found that the customary method of winning contracts was to bribe key officials of the regional purchase offices of the federal agency in charge. He began writing letters of protest to the government in 1974. These letters were ignored.

Then he began writing letters to the Washington *Post.* As a result of the *Post*'s revelations in 1978, based in part on Lowry's stories, the federal government finally eliminated fraud in the General Services Administration that was costing taxpayers an estimated $2.4 billion a year. The GSA administrator was fired, and the new one took contract allocation out of the well-hidden hands of the regional offices and centralized it in the spotlight of the head office in Washington.

The private individual with an angry tale to tell can go it alone, as Lowry did at first, taking the story directly to responsible government officials. Much too often, however, as Lowry found, there is no response. Lowry did better when he went to the media. But there, too, it is sometimes difficult for a private citizen to get attention. There are other places to bring complaints.

❖ ❖ ❖

41

Good government groups have long and honorable histories of achieving government reform. In 1907 underpaid young men in bowler hats counted bags of cement taken off their trucks by contractors for use on construction jobs for the city of New York. They were working for the Bureau of Municipal Research. Having painstakingly searched out the specifications for the work (which the city had been required to list in newspaper advertisements soliciting bids for the jobs), the young reformers knew how many bags of cement there were supposed to be. The Bureau of Municipal Research was in the process of proving that the city had paid for thousands of dollars' worth of supplies that were never delivered because of kickbacks to city employees. In consequence, three borough presidents would be forced to resign, and New York City became the first municipal government anywhere to institute a formal line-item budget, ending the practice of hiding from the public just how much of a given item the city was supposed to get for its money.

The Bureau of Municipal Research no longer exists, but other privately funded nonprofit good government groups, like the Citizens Union, Common Cause, and the Nader organizations, to name just a few, continue to expose and combat abuse brought to their attention by private citizens.

The battle against mortgage redlining in New York State, for example, was waged against the banks by the Public Interest Research Group, an organization affiliated with Ralph Nader, in cooperation with numerous community organizations. Starting in 1975, they exposed the refusal of local banks to grant mortgages in certain neighborhoods, even though much of the deposit money in the banks was from those very neighborhoods and even though some of the mortgage loans would have been sound investments. It was less troublesome for the banks to write off those neighborhoods entirely, when changing social conditions made some parts of them problematic, than to evaluate individual loan applications.

That the banks were permitted to do this reflected a failure of government policy, for the banks in question were mutual savings associations, under state charter and under the supervision of the State Banking Department. The Public Interest Research Group revelations received widespread publicity in the press, which did much to change public opinion.

Similar efforts by civic groups around the country resulted in congressional passage of the 1977 Community Reinvestment Act, which gave new teeth to anti-redlining efforts. By 1979 the efforts of the New York Public Interest Research Group and its allies had sparked sufficient vigor in the enforcement of this act so that mortgage terms, conditions, and availability in many of the formerly redlined neighborhoods began to compare favorably with suburbia.

The Public Interest Research Group is a large and well-run civic group. But any civic or neighborhood group—even garden clubs, church groups, block associations—can use similar methods to fight bad government. So can any individual. The obstacle for most individuals and groups is that success requires persistence and skill. It is not easy for a person with a full-time job and no time to spare to keep trying after writing six complaint letters and getting no response. It is not easy for a small organization with limited funds for legal and secretarial work—intended for gardening, helping the Boy Scouts, or whatever—to fight a bureaucracy committed to persisting in some terrible policy or practice. Therefore, organizations with people who have time and who know the workings of the law, the press, and the government have the advantage of better odds.

Still, victories can be won by combatants who are lacking these weapons. Sometimes it takes just one telephone call to a reporter to begin the process of scandal and reform. Indeed, a single outraged civilian from Washington, D.C., heard of Lieutenant Calley's shooting of innocent women and children. His telephone call to reporter Seymour Hersh started an investigation of the My Lai massacre. Hersh's revelations in the press would later help shock the American people into a clearer realization of the fruitlessness of continued efforts in the Vietnam War.

The press plays a crucial role. The citizen or civic group seeking reform is usually well served by media attention to the problem. In fact, reporters often begin the process on their own, without prompting from anyone. In recent years the most effective reformers of all have been journalists.

The role of Bob Woodward and Carl Bernstein of the

Washington *Post* in terminating the presidency of the unindicted co-conspirator in Watergate is history. No doubt they have inspired much of the reform movement in the United States since 1974. Reporter Don Bolles now belongs to history as well. His murder in 1976 by a hit man for the corrupt Arizona interests he was investigating brought a host of courageous reporters from all over the country to continue his work. They exposed numerous connections between Arizona politicians and notorious mobsters. Jack Anderson, Seymour Hersh, Jack Newfield, and Nick Pileggi are nationally known muckraking reporters who continue the tradition of their early-twentieth-century predecessors Lincoln Steffens, Upton Sinclair, Ida Tarbell, and the rest. Equally important to reformers are journalists whose names are not as well known but who are active on local issues.

A particular kind of politician now supplements the press in the investigation of government abuse. Sometimes citizens or civic groups bring the matter to the politician. Sometimes the politician begins the investigation on his or her own. The kind of politician needed is, first of all, usually a legislator.

Those in control of executive branches of government—mayors, governors, and Presidents—have a difficult time implementing major reforms. Their usual roles as compromisers among many powerful interests (unions, government bureaucracies, banks, ethnic groups, interest groups of all kinds) make it difficult for them to play the conflicting role of "reformer."

It is easier for a legislator, without executive responsibility, to play the role of the critic and to apply pressures to achieve reform. Only a few legislators are committed reformers, but their number is growing. On the national level William Proxmire of Wisconsin and Paul Tsongas of Massachusetts in the Senate, Anthony Toby Moffett of Connecticut, Les Aspin of Wisconsin, and Andrew Jacobs of Indiana in the House all are Democrats who criticize Democratic administrations as well as Republican. Many other activists, working at state and city levels, are far less prominent.

A legislator commands only the formal power to introduce legislation and to vote on bills. Depending on the closeness of the vote, the size of the legislative unit voting, and the influence of the legislator with his or her colleagues, this power may be more or less significant. This formal legislative power is sometimes relevant to reform efforts, as we shall see in our case study on the city auction process in Chapter 17. But even there, its significance was entirely subordinate to that of many more important factors.

More important are the *hidden* powers that accrue to public officials. These powers are what the legislator makes of them. One such is the advantage of heightened access to information. The legislator with an active office in the district he or she represents will learn a great deal about the way government agencies are operating because the public will come in to complain about them. The legislator with an active research staff will learn more than other people can about government operations from the government itself because agencies are quicker to answer questions posed by their funding sources, the legislators.

Another hidden power is that a legislator has greater access to the press as a public official than does a private citizen. A newspaper or television editor is likely to consider more favorably a press release from someone who represents a constituency than from a private individual. Having discovered an instance of dishonesty or inefficiency in government, a legislator may be able to identify and expose the problem in the press. This will, in turn, bring about public pressure on those responsible for the problem.

Finally, legislators have the power to hire staff members as watchdogs. No legislator today can afford, personally, to be a full-time watchdog against waste and abuse. Constituent service, community problems, and various legislative matters make too many inescapable demands. Staff members, however, may be able to develop skills as full-time reformers on behalf of the legislator. As more legislators investigate waste, mismanagement, or corruption in the executive branches of government, the role of the staff reformer grows.

The relationship between the staff reformer and the politician can be symbiotic. The politician is the one whose name gets into the newspaper as "exposing," "revealing," "disclosing," "charging" whatever the scandal is. Even with the best politician, the staff reformer gets relatively little credit for his or her work. Of course, those on the inside know: other politicians; sources; colleagues; members of the press; bureaucrats. Those politicians with relatively little self-confidence insist that their reformers remain as anonymous as possible.

But there are rewards even for reformers working for such politicians. The reformer's job, if done well and successfully, is one of the few opportunities in modern life to be a paid Don Quixote. Even the reforming politician, with all the courage and integrity it takes for that role, has to dilute the purity of his or her work of reform with the other, "political" things a politician must do. The reformer bears no such burden. Furthermore, the politician runs the political risk in larger measure: The politician may be defeated; the reformer may get another job with another reform politician.

Reformers on legislative staffs need not be lawyers. However, legal habits—requiring sufficient evidence and a clear chain of logical deduction from evidence for each allegation—play an important part in the reform process. If the legislator is not a lawyer, the staff reformer probably should be one.

A salary to do this kind of work, sharpened skills through practice in a variety of investigations, and enhanced access to the press as a result of political position are great advantages. The professional reformer as a member of a legislative staff is on the cutting edge of American politics today. Such professionals are well positioned to initiate important and effective investigations of government abuse and also to offer a place for citizens to take their own efforts to obtain reform.

3

How-to Guide to Reform

INVESTIGATIONS OF GOVERNMENT BEGIN in several ways. In rare instances reformers stumble over the evidence. One literal example was the spoiled food that New Yorkers stumbled over on the city streets (see Chapter 1). However, those who benefit from malfeasance are rarely so careless as to leave evidence lying around.

Once you, or the politician or organization you are working for, have acquired a reputation for fighting corruption, members of the public will step forward in increasing numbers to provide information. Once you have acquired a reputation for consistently protecting the confidentiality of sources, government employees will come forward in greater numbers and frequency.

A network inside the government begins to grow, composed of reformers and good sources, who remain in contact with one another. Each provides information that the others need and provides expertise when colleagues need such assistance.

Investigative reporters and reformers are often colleagues. The networks of private citizens and government employees working toward reform certainly include such reporters. Reporters sometimes reverse the usual flow of information and give you a tip to investigate. This happens only after the reporter and reformer have established a close working relationship. Even then it occurs only when the reporter is too busy to follow the lead personally.

* * *

Leads come in varying degrees of quality and detail. One may be no more than a hint: "You ought to look into the Department of Visibility—everyone there is on the take." At the other extreme, you may get a highly informative and well-organized presentation by a government employee or private expert who has already analyzed a situation and merely wants it exposed. It is more often a vague hint than a lucid analysis, and it is usually somewhere in between.

Usually investigative leads come from "sources." Sources are individuals who seek to bring a complaint of some kind to a reformer. They may be private individuals, like Lowry, the painter who helped expose the General Services Administration scandal, or government employees. They are of every degree of sanity, intelligence, lucidity, idealism, and honesty. Refreshingly often their motivation is idealism and honesty. Many government employees, especially those who have chosen a career in government for idealistic reasons, find their idealism frustrated by incompetence or dishonesty in the agency which employs them. When they fear that complaining "in house" will be useless and that criticizing the agency publicly will cost them their jobs, they sometimes find their way to a reformer whose name has been in the paper. In such cases confidentiality is of the utmost importance.

In other cases the source may have an ax to grind. He or she may be angry with the boss or the agency, justly or unjustly, and may reveal embarrassing information in the spirit of revenge. The source may be paranoid, but as Delmore Schwartz wrote, "Even paranoids have enemies." A somewhat insane source may still be correct.

After a number of years you begin to develop a nose for scandal, a sensitivity to programs or agencies which warrant investigation. Sometimes information obtained in one investigation will provide the basis for another, separate investigation. A name connected with a particularly bad participating agency in one scandal can, merely by appearing in connection with some new government program, provide a clue that it, too, warrants serious examination.

The first question, therefore, is evaluation of the lead. Can the facts be substantiated with the staff and resources available to you? If you are stuck with some technical controversy upon which professional opinion differs, it is usually not worth wasting your limited time and energy. For example, someone told me that certain fire department equipment was so inappropriate that only wrongdoing could account for its selection and purchase. Because I lacked the technical background necessary to understand the equipment, I could not have made a good evaluation or fair judgment of its appropriateness without spending an excessive amount of time on study and neglecting my other work. Therefore, I decided against becoming involved.

There are investigators who expose scandals without first proving that the matter is as they claim. During Holtzman's investigation of the summer food program an assemblyman decided to get into the act. Basing his charges on a list of food distribution sites which he didn't realize was obsolete, he charged that the B'nai Torah organization was ripping off funds by failing to deliver any lunches to a site needing 200 lunches a day. The site had been closed, and B'nai Torah had stopped receiving payment for it, three weeks earlier. The assemblyman's more general charges about B'nai Torah's bilking the government were quite accurate, of course, but his faulty presentation cost him credibility—and later a $6 million lawsuit against him by Rabbi Lieb Pinter of B'nai Torah. The assemblyman was overheard asking plaintively, "Why did Pinter sue me and not Holtzman?" The suit against him was later dropped presumably because B'nai Torah knew better than to expose its records to discovery, but only after the assemblyman suffered the embarrassment of the lawsuit's publicity.

Such careless "reformers" damage the credibility of more careful reformers and may hurt innocent individuals. Thus, the first step in an investigation is to determine whether a reasonable investment of time and energy can be expected to produce a definitive answer.

The next question is: Assuming you can prove the allegations, will your involvement be useful? This is a complicated matter. Often, well-known social or economic conditions underlie a problem which cannot be corrected without changes in these conditions. Such a problem is beyond the reach of the system of reform presented here. Our most potent weapon is the power to embarrass. Therefore, the most efficient use of your time is that which will result in the exposure of the most serious scandal. If the newspaper headline will read "Coruption!" the impact will be greater than if it merely reads "Waste in Government!" The headline will be bigger; the mayor will be more embarrassed; the public will be more outraged; the follow-up can include visits to the district attorney or the U.S. attorney. Something will probably be done to correct the situation.

The headline reading "City Wastes $1 Million in Silly Boondoggle" may be somewhat less dramatic, but it will suffice if no certifiable corruption can be documented. If the headline reads "Mismanagement"—i.e., "The program could do a better job if some intelligence were applied, as follows"—it had better come out on a very slow news day, or you will not get a headline. This type of scandal is certainly worth exposing, but it is by far the most difficult kind to do effectively—that is, to do and to have some real result come of it. Only the public relations genius of Assemblyman Charles Schumer enabled an important exposé of this type to receive any attention at all.

This was a highly technical analysis exposing the mismanagement of the Port of New York's railroad cargo facilities in 1977. Much of the economic fate of New York City rests on the fate of the port, and the port depended on these technical items. But they were very technical and thus, to the media, very boring. So Schumer billed the press conference at which the report was released as a "tugboat tour of New York's dying waterfront." The tugboat tour was provided, and the matter received sufficient coverage to engage public attention and to begin to generate solutions to some of the port's problems.

But the mismanagement scandal is the hardest to do. Thus, the second step is to assume you will succeed in proving the matters alleged. Then it is necessary to ask: Will a headline result? What will it say? Will it result in a public improvement? Is the significance of the improvement worth the opportunity lost of not being able to investigate something else? Your decision to investigate must depend on arriving at positive answers to these questions.

Once you have decided to begin an investigation, you must substantiate every fact required to support the conclusion, the headline that you envision. Almost invariably you will have to obtain information from the very agency you are trying to reform. To the extent possible, it is wise not to reveal the focus of your investigation to the agency. Otherwise, the agency will be warned of exactly what it must hide.

Precisely who in the agency you approach is quite relevant at times. If you approach the agency at the lowest level, the first clerk past the one who answers the telephone, that person may not know or care about the matter under investigation and therefore may not provide the information you seek. On the other hand, the clerk may not understand the sensitivity of the matter in question and may therefore be willing to supply information that higher officials might prefer to hide.

In some agencies, particularly those with much to hide, lower-level staff members are not permitted to answer questions. For example, shortly after the airing of three drug program scandals, largely based on information supplied to me by agency personnel, all further questions asked of New York City's Addiction Services Agency were referred to the agency's general counsel. This, of course, is known as locking the barn after the horse has been stolen.

An agency may insist that all requests for information be in writing. This may be either as a first line of defense for an agency that chooses not to cooperate or a reasonable response to assure that the communications of both parties will be a matter of record. In this latter respect, written requests and responses are helpful to you. They are at hand and can easily be supplied to a skeptical reporter or cited in the face of subsequent agency denials. However, at the beginning of research, and later, as matters come to a head and information is needed quickly, the response of "put the request in writing" is a time-consuming irritant. If you are engaged in several investigations at one time, you can wait for written responses for one investigation while you attend to other matters.

When your request is in writing, you may cite the state or federal freedom of information acts. (The state acts are applicable to city governments as well.) This has both advantages and disadvantages. The advantages are that the agency will know that you are not anxious to waste time waiting for a response because the acts require responses within stated periods.

The time period can be mentioned in the request letter. The agency is also on notice that you are aware of the legal right to information available to the public.

The disadvantages are that the seriousness of your inquiry is emphasized, thereby alerting the agency that a real investigation is under way. It can then refuse to supply the information by using any of the numerous applicable excuses in the freedom of information acts, such as the exception for internal memoranda.

If the agency refuses to comply with a request for information under the freedom of information acts, you may threaten to sue, under the appropriate provisions of the acts. If its excuse under the act is valid, it may ignore the threat of suit. Or it may comply, since even an unsuccessful suit may bring bad publicity to the agency.

Alternatively, reformers with legislative authority may threaten to subpoena necessary information. Again, it is bad publicity for an agency to become known as the subject of a subpoena.

I have used both threats and never had to carry out either. Execution takes much time and trouble. However, if the threat is merely a bluff, it may not be a credible threat for long. You must be prepared and willing to act.

The best source of information in an agency is an inside source who can easily and voluntarily—and unofficially and confidentially—provide you with copies of files. Sometimes, in the course of investigating an agency, a fresh inside source will arise. This new source is apart from the source of the initial lead. This may happen because the employee sees a long-awaited opportunity to "clean things up" or because he or she hates the agency or the boss. Or perhaps the employee is particularly farsighted, recognizes that the roof is going to fall in, and wants to be a survivor. He or she may decide that the reformer's side is the one to be on when the fall comes.

Information, even when available, is not always what it seems. So the next step is analysis. The reformer must look for patterns, contradictions, and inconsistencies. The winning bidder to supply asphalt to New York City in 1975 bid $18 a ton. Another bidder had bid $19.15 to New York, but only $14.15

to a smaller customer for the same product. Why bid higher to the bigger customer? If he didn't want the contract, why did he bid at all? The answer was that the bids were submitted to foster the illusion, not the reality, of competition. This discovery, with its implications of price-fixing, reverberated through the media and the asphalt industry and eventually resulted in major changes in the city's asphalt supply procedure, as will be shown later.

Because every investigation requires its own tools, specifically crafted to the subject matter, it is hard to generalize about the techniques of analysis. For one investigation you might have to go out onto the street for a few days to time buses to test Transit Authority claims regarding bus schedule performance. For another, you might have to call police departments in cities using cheap walkie-talkies to check your city's police department claim that only a more expensive brand is suitable for its needs. If police in comparable jurisdictions say the cheaper brands are just as good, then you know that you can raise hard questions about why your police demand such narrow specifications.

Finally, you must judge the significance of what you uncover. Is it a small sample of a large problem, or is it an isolated case? The first few dozen lunches carted away from summer food program sites might have reflected some minor management problems, but long before the 16,000 sandwiches were found dumped in the Bensonhurst lot, it had become clear that much more than minor mismanagement was involved.

Once you understand the scope of the problem, you can begin to devise solutions. These may be tougher competitive bidding requirements, unannounced inspections, transferring a program from one agency to another, canceling a contract, and so on. Together with exposing the problem, the reformer's responsibility is to propose at least an idea for a solution.

The next step is preparing the story for release to the press. The press is the single most powerful weapon of reform. This is not solely an American phenomenon. The Englishman E. L. Normanton, in *The Accountability and Audit of Government*, quotes a French opinion that "Nothing is more disagreeable to an official—and this applies with even greater emphasis to a politician—than the public exhibition of his weaknesses."

Always prepare a written press release, so that you have a written record of the charges. This is especially helpful later in case of threatened or actual suit for libel or other controversy. If you are a reformer working for a reform politician, the final version of the release should be prepared jointly by you, the politician, and the publicity professional, if one is available. It will be the politician's name that goes on the release. Therefore, it is essential that the politician is completely convinced of the accuracy and propriety of everything in it.

Even though you take every precaution to make certain that the charges are accurate, the individuals charged are not guilty of the exposed crimes until a jury returns a verdict. Therefore, if your allegations include criminal wrongdoing, you must preface such charges with modifying words like "apparently," "seemingly," "allegedly," and the like. For purposes of defense against libel suits, it is best to use such modifiers even when there are no criminal implications. The press may try to goad you into dropping such modifiers by dangling the prospect of better coverage if the charges are "stronger." Better coverage is not worth legal liability. You may eventually win the case in court, but your time is not best spent in preparation of a legal defense.

At the beginning all you can do is send the press release to the city desks of major newspapers and wire services and hope for the best. Hundreds of press releases cross these desks every day. Any given release is likely to be ignored. You can pray for a slow day or that your subject will arouse the interest of an assignment editor.

It is the job of newspaper personnel to sell newspapers and of radio and television personnel to attract and hold listeners and viewers. To the extent that an exposé will help the media do these things, its chances of coverage are improved. Packaging can make the difference. For television coverage and newspaper photo desks, a press conference designed to be visually interesting can save a story that is not otherwise especially juicy. An exposé of parking ticket quotas posed a problem for Assemblyman Charles Schumer. The subject had limited visual interest. So Schumer informed the press that at a news conference he would present anonymous witnesses behind a screen to conceal their identities. A photograph of three eerily silhouetted witnesses made the front page of the New York *Daily News.*

If a matter does not lend itself to visual presentation, it is usually sufficient to send out a press release. Busy reporters do not like to travel unnecessarily to a press conference simply to hear a politician talk. They refer to this phenomenon as the "talking head" story, as in the supposed headline "Talking Head Found on Top of Politician." Unless there is a reason to travel, something to see, reporters prefer to write from a press release delivered to their desks. Only if there is an important visual aspect to the story, or if the story has unusual dramatic potential based solely on the subject matter, is a press conference appropriate. An example of the latter would be the charging the mayor with accepting bribes and documenting the charges. Even if there is nothing interesting to see in the documentation, the inherent drama in such serious accusations justifies a press conference and visual coverage.

If a press conference is planned, advisories notifying the press of the time, location, and subject should be sent to the city desks of the newspapers and wire services. For example, "On Monday, April 10, at 10:00 A.M. on 10th Avenue and 3rd Street, Senator Smith will reveal that the chief of the Department of Visibility received a $10,000 bribe to permit the illegal operations of an obscurity-producing company. Senator Smith will make his disclosures in front of Scenic Gardens, now grossly obscured by a product of the company that gave the bribes." It is useful to send advisories to the assignment editors' desks at television and radio newsrooms, even though they use the wire services. Seeing an advisory on their desks as well as on the wire may help gain their attention. At the press conference, press releases should be distributed, and copies should also be delivered to media not represented at the conference.

In notifying the press of a conference or a release, don't oversell your stories, or you'll lose credibility for the future. As credibility grows, assignment editors become more and more responsive to stories emanating from a particular reformer. Also, relationships with reporters develop. If a reporter is regularly assigned to your area of operations and comes to know your work and respect it, he or she will come to regard you as a regular source and may even try to fight to cover your particular stories.

Sometimes it is useful to give a newsman an "exclusive"— that is, to give that reporter, and only that reporter, first crack at an exposé. This may be a good diplomatic maneuver with that one reporter, but it may alienate others. On the other hand, if reporters see a good exclusive that they didn't get, they may pay more attention to you in the future.

For the most part, however, these considerations make little difference. The quality of the story is what counts. Tactical factors, like exclusives, good relationships with reporters, and even good reputations with editors, do not count for much more than an edge with respect to coverage.

Distinctions of some kinds must be made among the media. It may not be worth extensive efforts to stress visual interest at the expense of the solid background information that helps win coverage in newspapers. Television, after all, is not primarily a news medium.

Many television viewers will turn off either their sets or their minds when the news comes on, unless it is particularly entertaining. Furthermore, those who do get their news from television may not be the opinion makers. People in a position to translate their indignation into political pressure for the changes you seek are more likely to get their news from newspapers, particularly from the best newspapers. To some extent, the Boston *Globe* is the newspaper for opinion leaders in Boston; the Washington *Post*, for opinion leaders in Washington; *The New York Times* fills this role in New York and to some extent in other cities.

Unfortunately it is particularly difficult to get *The New York Times* interested in covering a local story, even when the locality is New York. The *Times* sees itself as a national or international newspaper and has relatively little space to devote to scandals in city government. A city scandal that produces news stories over a period of weeks in other newspapers will eventually attract the attention of the *Times*. And, of course, if the scandal is truly enormous, the paper will cover it in any case. But hard as it is to "crack" the *Times*, once done, the matter grows enormously in the consciousness of the public. Even other media will give more respect to the story. The *Times* is, after all, the "newspaper of record."

Local press, however, can be quite sufficient to provide the political embarrassment needed to generate action. The principal newspaper in any city is obviously extremely important to the political leadership of that city. Occasionally newspaper publishers are too cozy with local politicians to publish revelations of their misbehavior. Such suppression, however, will serve to make the matter so much the more interesting for rival news sources. Local radio stations, for example, are often hungry for news items and can therefore bring competitive or indirect pressure on local newspapers.

It is all too easy for reformers to regard press coverage as the objective. For reformers of integrity, it is *not* the objective. It is only a tool to use in an effort to make government work better.

The principle underlying the efficacy of this tool is that government officials prefer not to be embarrassed. Bad publicity, with the credible threat of more bad publicity, can influence officials to change their actions. The failure of many scandal-exposing politicians to achieve real reform is attributable to their failure to provide a credible threat of *more* bad publicity. In such cases, the bureaucrats under attack correctly guess that the politician will be satisfied with a headline and will not pursue the matter further, especially if influenced in some way not to do so. The politician who is committed to achieving real reform and who understands the long-term benefits of a reputation for such commitment will at first be given the standard treatment but will become more successful as the credibility of the follow-up threats becomes better known.

To some extent, the fear that the reformer may inspire in the bureaucracy can create positive change without the use of any press at all. Depending on the relationship between the reformer and the politician as well as the degree to which either is interested in solving problems without getting publicity, the threat of giving a bureaucrat bad publicity may be enough to force the bureaucrat to change his or her ways.

I have used such threats to solve many problems, such as motivating the board of education to provide school bus transportation which was mandated for a handicapped child or improving the maintenance of city ambulances.

You may also be able to use the incentive of good press, rather than the threat of bad press. I helped encourage two city agencies to close a loophole in a real-estate-related area by hinting that I would praise them to the press if they adopted a cross-checking procedure with each other. They did adopt the procedure, and I did help them get good publicity for it.

However, basic press credibility is the power to provide bad press. The subject of a new investigation is more likely to fear your threat if stories of your recent exposés have found their way into the press. The press is also more responsive if you have a reputation for providing interesting, reliable information. And the public acquires an interest if you have already proved yourself adept at reform. Only a record of regular, successful use of bad publicity creates credibility.

Although exposure of misdeeds through the press is the primary threat, there are secondary threats as well. These depend on the nature of the scandal exposed. If criminal wrongdoing is involved, turning over relevant information to the district attorney or the U.S. attorney is useful. Another secondary threat is a call for the resignation of the bureaucrat involved. If the scandal is sufficiently embarrassing to an elected official with ultimate responsibility, he or she may choose to blunt the electoral impact of the scandal by firing or seeking the resignation of the bureaucrat immediately responsible. This is true whether or not the elected official is personally responsible in some way.

For example, widespread police corruption was uncovered in Chicago in 1960. The late Mayor Richard Daley is presumed to have known about the situation all along. Daley did nothing about it, however, until after the public exposé. At that point he replaced the police commissioner with a well-known expert on police reform, Orlando Wilson. The result of this "bold" and "forthright" move was that Daley *gained* political support, although it was his own police administration that was corrupt, and it had been at least partially his own fault.

Unless handled adroitly, scandal constitutes a threat to the reelection of the elected official. Usually the seriousness of the threat depends on how closely the elected official is linked to the scandal. Enough scandals in an administration, even without close links to an elected official, may jeopardize reelection possibilities in any case.

When the investigation is conducted under a legislative official, punitive or coercive legislation stands as an additional threat. Funding or jurisdiction may be withdrawn from a bureau by a legislative body sufficiently aroused. Legislative bodies may be aroused, of course, by voters demanding that their legislators do something about the scandal they've read about in the newspapers. The reformer stirs the press, which stirs the public, which stirs the politicians.

Follow-up is necessary. The press will respect the reformer and the politician who check six months later, and a year later, and two years later, to see whether the reforms promised by the administration in response to the exposé ever actually took place. If you find that the changes promised did not take place or were ineffectual, you may notify reporters, who are usually willing to write a follow-up story. This will benefit the reforming politician as well as the public.

When the bureaucracy knows that it will continue to be hit with bad publicity until it mends its ways, it will be far more anxious to change than when it thinks it can ride out the storm. In addition, you should keep in mind the other available forms of follow-up. These are corrective legislation, informal communication with elected officials with ultimate responsibility, reminders to prosecutors if they have a relevant role, and demands for the removal of incompetent officials.

Many or perhaps most problems in government have roots beyond bureaucratic inaction or malfeasance. Some fundamental problems cannot be solved without addressing economic or social conditions. To the extent that pressure placed on government over relatively short periods of months or even a few years cannot solve these problems, the techniques described here will fail. However, as cases in other chapters illustrate, surprisingly often these techniques succeed.

To sum up, the following principles are the logical premises underlying our system of reform:

 **Government officials can be embarrassed into doing what they ought to be doing.
 **When they are doing other than they ought, bad publicity can provide the necessary embarrassment.
 **Bad publicity for them can provide good publicity for the reformer. This motivates many politicians to engage in continued reform.
 **Press coverage has such allure to most people, including reformers, that it can supplant constructive change as the objective, undermining the reformer's effectiveness. This threat must be resisted. Press coverage is only a tool, not the goal.
 **Seasoned bureaucrats expect reformers to be satisfied with a headline. Thus, they may attempt to weather the storm when the initial public revelations come out. Therefore, it is important to establish a credible threat of additional bad publicity in order to force change.
 **Sometimes political forces protect, or benefit from, government abuses. The reformer must go forward with the exposure of important information that comes to light despite political considerations. Otherwise, political interference can stymie every investigation.
 **Since credibility is your major asset, it must not be wasted. No exposé, charge, or revelation should be made without proof beyond a reasonable doubt that the matter is as alleged.

A fairly uniform pattern emerges during the progress of most reform efforts utilizing our system:

1. THE LEAD: Investigations start with a "lead." Leads are usually derived from your own knowledge of government abuse or tips from other people, who may be private citizens or government employees.
2. EVALUATION: The lead must be evaluated. Is the problem one which exposure can help correct? Are the allegations provable? If so, do the scope of the problem

and the potential results of exposure make it worth the effort—including the cost of forgoing other investigative opportunities?

3. SUBSTANTIATION: If the lead is worth pursuing, basic information, preferably in documentary form, is needed. This is obtained by oral requests, written requests, requests under freedom of information acts, subpoenas, and inside sources with access to documents and a copying machine.

4. ANALYSIS: When the information is in hand, the facts may not mean what they seem to mean. Patterns, contradictions, and inconsistencies are the keys that unlock the mysteries and reveal the truth. Reports may be too complimentary; competitive bids may be too tightly competitive; ratios may be too disparate to be credible. Every investigation requires the crafting of a new set of tools for analysis. In later chapters, case studies convey the methods of analysis for specific situations.

5. SOLUTION: The reformer should offer a solution along with his or her disclosure of the problem. The solution must be geared to the problem; generalizations are of no use in this context.

6. PRESS: The power to effect change is largely dependent on the press, for the press provides the embarrassment to the malfeasor. If the investigation has been properly performed and the results have been properly publicized, you should be able to extract promises of reform.

7. FOLLOW-UP: Three weeks, six months, one year, two years later you must check to make sure that the changes were implemented and, if implemented, that they are working. Reporters are usually willing to write follow-up stories. The bureaucracy must be made aware that it will continue to be hit with bad publicity until it mends its ways. It is the credible threat of *continued* bad publicity that is most effective.

4

Plodding, Plodding

WHAT THE FOOD SCANDAL taught us was a rough structure to apply to any investigation: the lead, evaluation, substantiation, analysis, solution, press, and follow-up. Evaluating a lead can be the hardest step. Not all are as blatant as 16,000 sandwiches lying in a street. Often a lead is a vague hint, a tip from a stranger, or just a hunch about a situation that smells fishy. Tracking down such vague leads often requires hours of plodding, uninteresting work.

The three leads that involved me in city drug rehabilitation programs were vague, and collecting evidence took hours of dreary paper shuffling. Yet sticking to the system used in the food scandal resulted in important reforms.

By this time (1977) I had been appointed director and counsel of the New York State Assembly Subcommittee on City Management. I took the job on the condition that I could operate without concern for the impact of our work on sensitive political toes. Because 1977 was a mayoral election year, and the mayor was a candidate for reelection, questioning the management competence of his administration seemed timely. How the city was monitoring its drug abuse treatment programs was one aspect of the question.

I had little to go on except that suspicions had been surfacing about one such program. Previous investigations had revealed some strange goings-on in a drug treatment program named SERA—the Spanish acronym for Hispanic Association for a Drug-Free Society. Among other things, two of SERA's

63

directors had been apprehended by the police for throwing a fire bomb into an empty bus owned by SERA. Yet the program's director, Roberto Munoz, had refused to be a complainant on behalf of SERA. Munoz's record included a conviction in February 1976 for conspiracy to use explosives and to extort. Another source of mistrust about this group's operation was the building SERA had bought with taxpayer money. The building had been bought by Munoz's lawyer's corporation for $75,000 and resold to SERA on the same day for $325,000. The neat profit of $250,000 in one day was paid for by taxpayers.

Was SERA an isolated rotten apple in the barrel? Or was there a pattern of such abuse in the city's overall drug program?

I had a second lead that hinted the latter might be true.

Before leaving Holtzman's office to join the subcommittee, I had reviewed a preliminary list of sponsors applying to participate in the 1977 summer food program. On this list was a familiar name—Alfred Calloway. In 1976 Calloway had been director of Bedford-Stuyvesant Youth-In-Action, one of the sponsors that had lost government funding after our investigation of the food program. One of our memoranda had noted that Calloway, when asked by the government to submit proper documents on his operation, "preferred to shout obscenities over the telephone." Given its dismal record in the 1976 program, Bedford-Stuyvesant Youth-In-Action had the good sense not to apply under its own name for the 1977 summer food program. Instead, an application, listing Alfred Calloway as director, came from a group called Federation of Addiction Agencies (FAA), a drug abuse treatment program under contract with the city.

My third lead came from a confidential source who lived in Bedford-Stuyvesant, a poor community in Brooklyn. This source, whose information had consistently proved reliable, considered FAA a highly problematic entity that had survived primarily because of its political protection. The chairman of the board of FAA was a good friend of a city councilman, and this councilman's son had been on the board of directors until 1977. The chairman of the board of FAA turned out to be another name familiar to me—Richard Habersham-Bey. During the food program scandal of 1976 he had run one of the tours purporting to show how well the food programs were being operated (see page 25). Habersham-Bey was later found guilty of fraud in embezzling poverty program funds. The director of the FAA program happened to be one of Bedford-Stuyvesant's two representatives to the Council Against Poverty, the citywide poverty fund distributing body.

Unfortunately our source did not know any details of what FAA might be doing wrong or whether it was failing to provide the services for which it was paid. With these leads, however, I began to investigate FAA.

First, under the state Freedom of Information Act, our subcommittee requested permission from the city's Addiction Services Agency to review its drug program contract files. In order not to telegraph a particular interest in FAA and perhaps trigger a cover-up, our letter requested copies of all the contract files, not just those of FAA. The response was an invitation to visit the Addiction Services Agency and go through the files, which took up several rooms of filing cabinets. I accepted and, of course, made a beeline for the files of FAA.

I spent nearly two weeks opening drawer after drawer and searching through folder after folder. The stack of documents I had to comb through and take notes on was more than four feet high. After putting in a full day in the Addiction Services Agency's file rooms, I'd return to my own office to spend several more hours analyzing what I'd found. It all paid off because I found some astonishing information.

Two years earlier, in 1975, FAA had been audited. The auditors noted that incomplete files made a thorough audit impossible. However, even on the basis of the limited data available, they were able to identify more than $100,000 in improper expenditures.

The audit had been performed for the FAA's funding source, the federal Model Cities program, which became a national fiasco in its own right. In May 1975 Model Cities officials had informed the Addiction Services Agency that FAA should be forced to replace funds spent on ineligible items and otherwise correct the problems exposed by the audit. In December 1975 the Addiction Services Agency's general counsel asked its acting fiscal director what action, if any, had been taken. Our subcommittee asked this question again in April 1977. No answer was ever provided.

FAA's contract with the city authorized a budget of $740,000 a year for the drug abuse treatment program. The funding level was supposed to be geared to the program's contractual capacity, the number of patients the program was designed to treat. The National Institute on Drug Abuse recommended funding of about $5,000 per residential patient per year, and about $1,800 per outpatient. FAA's initial plan called for 100 residential clients and additional outpatients. This plan was buried deep inside about 100 pages of contractual "boilerplate," or standard legal language.

Finding those clients should have been no problem for FAA. The Brooklyn neighborhoods the program had been designed to serve—Bedford-Stuyvesant, Brownsville, and East New York—may lack many things, but there was no shortage of addicts presumably available to drug program outreach efforts.

A drug program did not immediately have to meet its contractual capacity, for the capacity was a goal that outreach efforts into the community were supposed to achieve eventually. Only after a few years, when no significant strides toward capacity were achieved, did the justification for a high level of funding wear thin.

How close did FAA come to its goal of 100 residential clients plus outpatients?

The files included monitoring reports, filed by city agency monitors who visited the drug programs in contract with the city. The visits were made quarterly and were announced in advance. The reports on FAA were rather complimentary, always explaining the difficulty of providing services. They reported that the program had about 30 residential patients in treatment but was trying to bring in more.

It seems that after many such reports the contractual capacity—but not the funding—was reduced to a level more commensurate with the number of clients in treatment. After FAA had failed for years to treat 100 patients, the city agency appears to have decided that 60 patients was a more appropriate goal. Although in later contracts FAA's capacity was reduced to 60 residential clients, this was not a meaningful decision because funding was not decreased. Funding continued at the $750,000-a-year level.

In reading the monitoring reports, I noticed strikingly similar phrases used from one report to another. Those phrases were noteworthy in that they did not sound as if their author were evaluating the program but rather were defending it. For example, the comment "the agency lends a helping hand whenever the need arises" appeared on page 4 of every report from January 1975 through January 1976.

As my suspicions grew, I became increasingly friendly with a middle-level executive at the Addiction Services Agency and began to ask him questions about the monitoring process. He conceded that "some" of the reports "may" not have been written by the monitor, but by FAA itself, over the monitor's name. Gradually, as the executive grew to trust me, he became more helpful. Finally, he dug out of the files the one report on FAA written by a different monitor.

This monitor counted beds for residential patients and found only seventeen. Noting previous census reports of sixty patients by FAA, this monitor wrote, "the program should strive to report their weekly census accurately. The figures reported are grossly out of line with fact." Nonetheless, after the Addiction Services Agency learned of the low client census, it approved FAA for an additional ten months at $640,000!

The solution to this problem was obvious: Cancel the contract, turn its responsibilities over to other existing programs, and devise screening and monitoring techniques to prevent such abuses in the future.

On Tuesday, April 19, 1977, the chairman of the subcommittee and I paid a surprise visit to FAA's residential treatment facility in Brooklyn. We had invited numerous reporters and television cameras. The New York Times article the next day, entitled "Brooklyn Drug Facility's Outlay Is Put at $45,000 a Year a Patient" noted that "there were four addicts at the Hopkinson Avenue facility yesterday during Mr. Schumer's visit."

The next day the program's director denied any padding of client census records. Two days later, on April 22, we prepared to announce that we had turned over eight sworn affidavits to the U.S. attorney alleging that the client census at

FAA was padded regularly and consciously at the director's request. These affidavits were the fruit of the initial publicity about the scandal. Former patients and staff of the program had called to offer the subcommittee congratulations and to add their own stories. I had taken down those stories in the form of affidavits.

The exposé got wide coverage in print and television. The *Post* ran an editorial lambasting the city's lackadaisical role. On April 23, the *Post*'s Murray Kempton added:

> Yesterday, the City's Addiction Services Agency halted its $75,000 a month grant to a Brooklyn treatment center after duly blushing at the revelation of Assemblyman Charles Schumer of Brooklyn that its costs were running $45,000 a year per junkie. Capo de tutti i capi from here to Union City Carmine Galante may be; but what hope of future profit can he have when he does not command a solitary button man competent to write an application for a federal grant?

The immediate need for further follow-up was somewhat vitiated, for as we prepared our announcement on April 22, officials of the Addiction Services Agency were making an announcement as well: FAA had been given thirty days' notice of the termination of its contract. Its seven-year spree was over.

5

A Little Old-fashioned Detective Work

GLORIA LAWRENCE, a diffident fortyish black woman, appeared in our subcommittee office several weeks after the Federation of Addiction Agencies (FAA) exposé to suggest that we investigate another drug abuse treatment program. The place was Logos Centers, Inc., where she had worked as a fund raiser.

The story she told gave us the opportunity to play detective in a way that fulfilled our childhood dreams of sleuthing. The tools of the detective are the phone, the mails, the eyes, the car, and the feet—usually in that order. Somehow, though, it is the last—on-the-scene presence and personal surveillance—that feels the most like detective work. Once in a while a case requires this type of footwork.

For several weeks after an investigative body such as our subcommittee draws attention to itself through an exposé, disgruntled people telephone or drop by. Such individuals imagine that their own personal vision of a perceived injustice will receive a sympathetic hearing, and perhaps redress, at the hands of an agency that seems to them to have corrected some comparable injustice. Some of these people will be unreliable or unstable, and their allegations may be unprovable or imagined. How much to believe is always the problem. Nevertheless, any source, particularly a disgruntled former employee, is worth your time. You can only try to hide the fact that you are listening with a strong dose of skepticism.

Even the better sources often provide an incredible jumble of information. Complaints and criticisms may be so mixed up that it's difficult to determine exactly what's being said. Some of this was true in Gloria Lawrence's case.

At first, Gloria didn't sound all that credible to me. A few things she said, though, were intriguing and might, after some investigation, be subject to substantiation.

She began with tales of real estate shenanigans. Logos Centers, Inc., was paying what *might* have been excessive rents to people who *might* have been in a less than an arm's length relationship with the program. These were public funds; if the program was claiming in its budget X dollars of rent a month, and if that figure was excessive for the space it was getting, it was possible that the landlord was kicking back some of the rent to the program directors—in their private capacities.

Secondly, Gloria made some amazing allegations which, if true, were real bombshells: that the program had bought stocks on the stock market and luxury cars for the personal use of the directors with drug program funds. These things, of course, would be difficult to prove, but they were very specific, and this caught our attention.

Following the lead in this case would be difficult, though. As a result of the embarrassment our FAA exposé had caused the city's Addiction Services Agency, it was being very cautious about providing access to its documents. It forbade us to search its files as we had before. Of course, we could have filed a Freedom of Information lawsuit, but then I'd have been spending my time in court instead of doing an investigation.

When I explained these matters to Gloria, she proved to be intelligent and resourceful. She thought awhile and then said that she had a friend who still worked in the Logos accounting office. This friend was also very angry at the way the program was being run and the dishonest tactics used. The friend, therefore, might be able to provide documentation. There is nothing better than an inside source; if someone is cooperating on the inside and slipping out information, the investigator is ideally supported.

Over the next few weeks I kept demanding documentation

from Gloria Lawrence, and she in turn would call her friend in the program. I kept pestering her. She kept saying, "Isn't this enough?" and I'd say, "No, we have to prove our charges." For the real estate information, we needed only the addresses of the buildings in the Bronx and of some land in Rockland County used by the program. For the Bronx real estate we went up to the Bronx county clerk and did a title search; for Rockland County we contacted the county clerk by phone. But for the stocks, we needed to know exactly which stocks had been purchased, and we needed the name of the stockbroker. And for the cars, we needed dealers, serial numbers of the sales receipts, and parking locations.

Gloria's friend finally procured for us a record of the stock transaction, and we called the broker to explain that it was partly a matter of record since I already had the customer's own slip. We had subpoena power, but we preferred that he cooperate with our investigation. He told us that the purchase of stock had indeed been made by Logos Centers, Inc.

As for the real estate, Logos claimed to have paid $60,000 a year in rent for an old hotel in Rockland County that its landlord had purchased for $310,000 in 1970. In 1976 the property was foreclosed upon for the $240,000 the landlord still owed on the unpaid mortgage. If Logos was really paying $60,000 a year in rent, it was hard to understand why the landlord couldn't meet the mortgage payments. Or was Logos putting in a claim for $60,000 to the city but using the money for something else?

The rent on the program's Bronx facility was listed as $30,000 a year. The landlord for that facility had paid $13,000 in cash for the property in 1970, plus annual mortgage payments of $18,200 for the first two years and $11,000 thereafter. The landlord would therefore have made a return on his investment of 91 percent before 1973, and more than 140 percent thereafter, before expenses. Even with a reasonable amount deducted for expenses, this constitutes a really wonderful rate of profit—paid for by the taxpayer, courtesy of the drug program—if, indeed, the landlord kept all of this sweet deal to himself, without sharing with the program or its directors.

We reported all this, but the press virtually never mentioned it, although it was by far the most substantively significant part of the story.

What was most dramatic and colorful, and would be clearest to the public, was, of course, the car purchase, and that's where some good old-fashioned detective work came into play.

At long last, I got from Gloria's friend the serial numbers of the three cars which she had read off the vouchers from the office files. The vouchers proved that the cars had been bought with program funds. And these were very interesting cars: One was a brand-new Buick Electra 225 with gold pinstripes, purchased for $9,000, which in 1977 was a great deal of money for a car. Although the other cars were cheaper, each had an AM-FM stereo tape deck. We called up the seller of the cars to double-check that the purchases were made in the name of Logos Centers, Inc. They were. Since people aren't usually very close to their car dealers, we weren't worried that word would get back to Logos that we were investigating. Next, we called a contact in the motor vehicles department, who, on the basis of the cars' serial numbers, gave us license plate numbers from the department computer. This is public information but not usually given over the phone.

We would achieve real drama, and thus focus attention on our story, if we could stand in front of a car and point to it. We had to show that the cars were *not* used for business purposes, that they were for the *private* use of the directors of the program. We wanted to show not only that the program directors had spent much too much for the cars—they didn't need a Buick Electra—but that they weren't even using them for anything faintly connected with the drug program.

When you seek funds from a government agency to run a drug program, it certainly doesn't expect you to use that money to buy a new Buick Electra 225. Even if you ask for private contributions, you are misrepresenting your intentions if you later use the money for a fancy car. That is fraud.

The real gumshoe work was finding the cars—physically going out and finding them. In order to do this, we had to find out where the directors lived and where they parked their cars. One lived in the Bronx and regularly took the subway to work. I found one car parked outside his house. This was a car bought with program funds, of course, and clearly was not being used for drug program work. However, this car was not a particularly fancy one, so it was not adequate for our visual purposes.

Our real quarry was the gold pinstriped Buick Electra. According to Gloria's friend, the director who drove the Buick parked it in any one of several garages in the morning. I was not optimistic. The drug program headquarters was located near Forty-fifth Street and Sixth Avenue, an area with loads of parking garages. I spent two days walking around parking garages, occasionally slipping the attendant a few dollars to let me walk through his garage and look at all the cars.

I did not expect to find it. But I did. I didn't know for a fact that it would still be there when we were ready to do a press conference. But we had already established the case: We had found that one in the garage and the other one at the employee's home in the Bronx. The third we were never able to locate.

On the morning of the press conference, May 20, after we had sent out an advisory saying that we would "show a $9,000 luxury car purchased with drug program funds," I was pretty nervous—the car might not be there. The press conference was scheduled for about noon. At 9:00 A.M. I went to the garage, gave the attendant the usual tip, and asked him if the car was there. It was. I said, "We're going to want access to this car at about twelve o'clock," and gave him another couple of dollars. He didn't ask any questions.

At noon we were there, along with reporters and photographers from the *News*, the *Post*, and television stations. By the time we left, about three hours later, the New York *Post* had come out, and as we rode the subway back to our office, we saw the front pages turned to us as passengers read the inside pages. The front page said, "Drug Funds Used to Play Market," and on page 2 was a picture of us, pointing to the car. The *Times* had the picture the next day.

Largely because of our investigation, the state concluded an audit of the program about three months later with the recommendation that it be taken away from its own management and turned over to a well-respected program. This happened.

* * *

One nice thing for us about the Logos exposé was that it provided a racial balance: FAA was a black-run program; the next program we exposed was Hispanic-directed; but Logos was directed by middle-class whites.

Our exposé of this program got far more press coverage than our exposé of FAA, and FAA was far, far worse. But the press loved the good visual in the Logos story. I resented the fact that the press gave this story so much play on that basis, when the FAA directors—proportionately to their offenses—deserved much more embarrassment, and the Logos directors, somewhat less. But the outcomes were appropriate: FAA was closed altogether; Logos was merely turned over to other management.

It is sometimes hard to retain a balanced point of view toward the press; coverage like that provided to the Logos story may at first irritate, but often finally seduces. There is a danger of going for a story like this one instead of perhaps more substantive and significant matter. But there was good enough reason for us to have pursued the Logos investigation. What we were doing with the drug programs was demonstrating that SERA—the earliest drug program scandal to be uncovered—was not just a rotten apple in the barrel. The city's drug program agency, Addiction Services Agency, was incompetent across the board in monitoring the programs and preventing abuse.

Indeed, the New York *Post* carried an editorial the next day noting that "abuses in the city's drug treatment program have become a depressing recurrent story in our newspaper, sort of a sick comic strip of local ripoff artists and incompetent officials riding the backs of addicts who urgently need help."

Our job was not done. To solve the underlying problems, and not merely to correct individually problematic programs, we had to reform the management of the city's drug abuse treatment programs. With the editorial support of the newspapers, we were now in a position to do so.

In the next few weeks we devised a series of fourteen guidelines for the city's Addiction Services Agency to apply to institute a policy of strict accountability. They would require unannounced monitoring visits to each program site at irregular intervals, funding to be limited to a formula based on objective data, and detailed annual budget justifications for each program to be made available for public inspection.

In May the mayor had ordered the takeover of the city's drug agency by the health department. In June we released our guidelines with the warning, reported by the *Daily News* on June 27, that the takeover could constitute "a meaningless bureaucratic reshuffling, vulnerable to the same abuses and scandal that plagued the ASA," unless reforms were instituted.

Over the next few months the new drug program officials worked with us on all the major reforms we sought—and they implemented twelve of our fourteen guidelines. Our continued monitoring of the drug programs under the new agency's jurisdiction turned up no serious problems.

6

Sometimes It Takes Awhile

In 1970, THE YOUNG LORDS, a radical Puerto Rican organization born in the protest movements of the late 1960's, took over Lincoln Hospital. Lincoln was a municipal hospital in the South Bronx, a poor Hispanic neighborhood. The Young Lords, who felt the hospital was not adequately meeting the community's needs, made a variety of demands for improved services.

The demands seemed justified, and a number of them were met. In fact, pressure from the Young Lords contributed to the construction of new hospital buildings, completed in 1976. The city had a novel situation—a municipal hospital over which a radical citizens' group exercised protective custody.

In this situation, with the community supportive of the improvements made and with some city officials nervous about angering the Young Lords, monitoring of the hospital's programs by appropriate agencies was not always forceful. This left the field open for exploitation by certain Hispanic community leaders.

The same forces that proved an obstacle to effective monitoring by city agencies confronted us, too, when, in 1977, our Subcommittee on City Management came to investigate mismanagement of a drug program at Lincoln Hospital. As a result, this case took an extraordinarily long time to resolve. Part of the problem was that we felt this program, with good management, was very worthwhile. Yet our attempts at reform threatened to kill the drug program altogether. So we found ourselves simultaneously exposing and fighting to save the same program.

One of the Young Lords' priorities after the hospital take-over was the establishment of a drug abuse treatment program. Officially titled the Lincoln Hospital Detoxification Program, it was known informally as Detox and was initially funded by the city's Addiction Services Agency.

My interest in Detox had been aroused while I was re-searching another drug program at the Addiction Services Agency. One of the agency's staff members, frustrated by cor-ruption in the city's drug programs, urged me to look into Detox. This suggestion was corroborated by a friend, a con-gressional aide, who had heard that Detox was tied into what we called the Velez Empire. Components of this empire were community organizations in the South Bronx that were linked in some way to City Councilman Ramon Velez. Indeed, we later learned that the board of directors of Lincoln Hospital was dominated for a long time by a man who also served as representative from the Velez-controlled South Bronx Com-munity Corporation to the Council Against Poverty, the agency then responsible for allocating the city's antipoverty funds.

I was additionally intrigued when I discovered that the di-rector of Detox was Luis Surita. Surita was a name I had come across before—he had been a staff member of SERA (see Chap-ter 4), a scandalous drug program run by Velez's henchman Roberto Muñoz.

I was therefore not surprised when our investigation showed that essentially, under Surita's direction, Detox had wasted at least $2 million of city funds, treated fewer than half the pa-tients it contracted for, and engaged in numerous other impro-prieties.

In fact, although my investigation did not begin until 1977, it seemed that suspicion of mismanagement at Detox had arisen at least by 1973. From early 1971 to early 1973 Detox had been funded by the city's Addiction Services Agency. However, in 1973, the state's drug program agency informed the agency that it would not approve any more payments to Detox unless Detox began to submit the required applications, information on how many patients it was treating, and other data. Detox officials refused to comply.

Nevertheless, the Detox program was not canceled. Instead, from 1973 to 1975 it appears that the city's Health and Hospitals' Corporation (HHC) "fronted" about $¾ million a year to Detox, somehow thinking that Detox would eventually comply with the state's requests and that the state would then reimburse HHC for the money for which Detox would have retroactively qualified. However, in 1975 HHC apparently realized that it would not be reimbursed. HHC then informed Detox that funding would cease.

Surita promptly brought a delegation from Detox to HHC headquarters for a demonstration. This resulted in the destruction of some furniture and, some allege, the physical strangling of a key HHC vice-president by a Detox employee until the HHC official agreed to restore funding. Whether or not the latter actually occurred, funding was restored.

On April 28, 1977, we released our report on Detox. We noted that the Addiction Services Agency's records of the program indicated that Detox charged the city more than four times the average city rate for methadone detoxification (about $261 per patient as compared with the normal clinic rate of $57 per patient). Also, it used medically unjustified, dangerous, and questionable techniques. Finally, it refused to provide records to verify alleged client treatment. Part of what the city funded was Surita's "political education" of patients, which was included in the Detox treatment program.

We noted that Surita's concept of political education, illustrated by the following passage in an Addiction Services Agency monitoring report, was hard to accept:

> Clients, despite the fact that many of them are on welfare, are often called upon to donate money to the freeing of "Political Prisoners." We observed one counselor at a P.E. [Political Education] class who had just been bailed out of jail with funds collected from the clients. He had come to thank them for their support. While there, he described how he had become a "Political Prisoner." Apparently, while under the influence of alcohol ("and a little reefer") he had bumped into a little girl on the street. When her father angrily confronted him, the counselor defended himself with a knife which he had in his boot. . . .

But we noted that Detox was providing effective treatment

for some, a difficult job in the South Bronx under any conditions. We thought that it had the potential to become an excellent program. In short, we told the city that closing the program, a simple solution, was the wrong solution. The right solution, making the program disciplined and accountable, was much harder.

We had been accustomed to dealing with the Addiction Services Agency, which could be embarrassed into reform. The funding agency here, however, was now HHC, and we were to find it much thicker-skinned.

For the next three months our repeated letters and telephone calls to HHC went unanswered. In August, however, a confidential source at HHC told us that it was doing its own—top-secret—audit of Detox.

In September we obtained audiences with top HHC officials, including its president, by threatening to release this audit. Actually, unknown to the HHC officials, we had not been able to obtain a copy of the audit. But we hoped the threat would be effective because we knew the audit had to have been extremely critical of Detox. The ruse worked. Because it thought we had the audit, HHC supplied us with its "latest draft," apparently a slightly less inflammatory document than the draft it thought we already had. HHC officials begged us not to release this document.

In October they continued trying to dissuade us from releasing the audit. HHC's arguments and our reactions reflected the unusual situation at Lincoln Hospital. Initially we were willing to concede that HHC understood the situation better than we did, and we therefore acceded to its request that we not make waves. HHC said it was in the process of negotiating with Detox to move addicts from the seventh to the first floor of Lincoln Hospital. A move against Detox should be postponed until this was done since any move by militants using physical force could be more easily "contained" on the first floor.

HHC also knew that we felt the record required that Surita be removed from his post. So it warned us that any open move against Surita should also be delayed until Detox was relocated. Otherwise, it said, firing Surita would result in "bloodshed."

At first we were willing to go along. However, as weeks

passed and Detox was moved to the first floor, the "militants" initiated no actions whatsoever. The move was quite peaceable. We began to have intimations that the physical danger from the Detox crew was imaginary.

Also, HHC now claimed that it had relieved Surita of administrative responsibilities, although it permitted him to remain at Detox. Given Surita's history, it was not credible to us that he could remain at the program and not run it.

After failing to reach agreement with HHC on the firing of Surita or the release of the audit, we released it ourselves on November 14, 1977.

The audit was an interesting document. It did more than corroborate our findings. It noted that the program was reimbursed for over $1 million in unsubstantiated payroll costs, that payroll checks were cashed in Puerto Rico during days a recipient was signed in as working at the program in the South Bronx, and that on a given and not atypical day, out of forty-five employees, twenty-three were absent and nine were late.

Michael Rosenbaum of the *Post* covered the story in a straightforward manner. To our astonishment, David Medina of the *Daily News* began his article by saying:

> [HHC] "yesterday rebutted charges of outrageous waste and mismanagement leveled against it . . . for its operation of the Lincoln Medical Center's Detoxification Unit. . . . "There were a number of discrepancies, but nothing approaching the $1 million in unsubstantiated payroll costs cited by Schumer," a spokesman for the corporation said. "Frankly, we don't know where he got that figure."

The figure came from the first sentence of HHC's own audit, as the unnamed HHC spokesman, the public relations man, must have known.

We had supplied a copy of the audit to Medina along with our press release. But after we read the article and questioned Medina, he said that he had never read the audit. When we confronted him with its statement of the $1 million "discrepancy," he remained unmoved. His story remained uncorrected and probably blunted the impact of our release.

Reform of Detox would have to wait for another day.

On taking office January 1, 1979, the city's new mayor pledged to eliminate those who profiteered off the misery of the poor. We, meanwhile, awaited developments at the city's department of investigation, to which we had forwarded copies of the audit and our request for investigation. When nothing happened, we called on the Office of Drug Abuse Services, the state drug abuse program licensing agency, to refuse relicensing to Detox unless it adopted key reforms—first and foremost, the removal of Surita.

The state agency hemmed and hawed for nine months, promising us that it would crack down but allowing itself to be taken in by HHC's promises. What shocked us into renewed public action was the Office of Drug Abuse Services' report to us that HHC had made, in the state agency's judgment, a very meaningful pledge: that it would place Surita under the administrative control of a Lincoln Hospital official. HHC had attempted to buy time from us with precisely the same pledge eight months earlier.

The state agency claimed to be shocked when we explained this but still refused to take any definitive action.

On November 27, 1978, we released what would be our third and final attack on Detox, a press release headlined "HHC, State Drug Agency Protect Rip-off Drug Program Through Years of Continuing Scandal."

The New York Times, after ignoring our charges concerning Detox over the previous eighteen months, now made up for it with a photograph of our subcommittee chairman criticizing the program on the first page of its second section and a massive 700-word article in explanation.

The next day's *Times* carried the follow-up story on page 1. The mayor, according to the article, "said he had assumed that the drug unit had been removed from the hospital last summer and that he was surprised to find it was still there when he read yesterday's editions of *The New York Times*. 'I had been told that it was no longer there,' [the mayor] said. 'This time I'm going to make sure that it goes forthwith.'"

At the mayor's orders, Detox in its entirety was evicted from Lincoln Hospital to the accompaniment of a police guard armed with crowbars, wire cutters, and sledgehammers, and Surita was fired on the spot. Other program officials were told that they would be reassigned to other jobs. It looked as if Lincoln Detox were finished.

This was not our goal then, and had never been our goal. We had no desire to throw out the baby with the bathwater. We had always praised the work of the Detox medical director, Dr. Michael Smith, and knew he needed the context of the program. But now even Mike Smith thought we were trying to destroy the program, and we began to be victims of bad press.

In a December 18 article in the *Village Voice*, former Young Lord (and then *Village Voice* reporter) Pablo Guzman repeated unfair and incorrect Detox staff accusations that we had "wooed" Smith—unsuccessfully—only because he was "white and a doctor" and "therefore more likely to operate a program less revolutionary and closer to their liking."

Meanwhile, however, we were working hard to make sure that Detox would survive. The new director of Lincoln Hospital, Joseph Cintron, was a fair man who was skeptical but nonetheless willing to give our plan a chance—that is, to see if Detox could be whipped into line. With his help, we fought for and won a written commitment from HHC to continue to fund the program—on a smaller scale, without Surita, and subject to tight administrative control. Cintron brought in a special administrator from Chicago with a reputation for toughness.

In June 1979 Mike Smith called me to thank me for our efforts, which he credited in large part for great improvements in the program. It is a rare and wonderful thing to be thanked by the subject of your exposé. The program was then treating 150 to 200 addicts a day. It used no methadone, but strictly acupuncture and counseling. It was the subject of a laudatory article in the briefly revived *Look* magazine. Cintron, at first skeptical of its salvageability, had high praise for its improvement and performance. At long last, we had won.

7

Being Taught Islam

"HERE IS A JOB—twenty dollars a week, ten seconds of work. Just sign the back of this fifty-dollar government check each week, hand it back to me, and I'll give you twenty dollars."

The above is only a slight caricature of how the Summer Youth Employment Program (SYEP) was once run in New York City. SYEP, funded by the federal Comprehensive Employment Training Act, was intended to provide classroom and on-the-job training as well as job placement for unemployed youth.

The theory of SYEP was that private nonprofit community organizations, or sponsors, were supposed to provide work for unemployed poverty-stricken youngsters fourteen to twenty-one years of age. Salaries for these youths were paid for by the federal government. The goal was to accustom these young people to work habits and the work ethic, to make them generally more attractive to future employers, and thus to achieve a long-term amelioration of unemployment among the poor.

In reality, however, many of the sponsors' programs were spurious. While it is not clear that any sponsor provided "jobs" precisely like that described above, no-show jobs, kickbacks, and nepotism were so widespread as to be characteristic.

Evidence of corruption was so strong that SYEP was being investigated simultaneously by Congresswoman Elizabeth Holtzman, by the Subcommittee on City Management, which I had joined since leaving her office, and by the city comptroller's office. We soon discovered that the names of SYEP sponsors were familiar from earlier investigations of other scandalous antipoverty programs.

For instance, one SYEP sponsor was Bedford-Stuyvesant Youth-In-Action, an organization we had run across during our probes of summer food programs and drug treatment centers. In fact, we had found contractual connections between Youth-In-Action and each of three other major corrupt antipoverty groups. Youth-In-Action was the parent organization of an almost completely fraudulent drug abuse treatment program at the same site as a summer food program and an employment program. Incredibly, under SYEP funding, sixty-three youths were allocated to "work" at the drug program here in the summer of 1976, when the patients numbered at most seventeen and the site already had a full-time staff of thirty-six.

Exactly what work the SYEP participants performed here was therefore somewhat unclear. It seems, however, according to affidavits submitted to our subcommittee, that they helped *sell* the needy children's summer lunches to members of the general public who happened to be passing by.

This would go somewhat beyond some of the more typical job descriptions for the SYEP assignments that Youth-In-Action provided. Youth-In-Action, which had been given $1.6 million in federal funds for 3,691 placements in 1976—the largest such program in the country—had assigned its youth to such jobs as "being taught Islam," being directed to "write, read," and "go on trips and attend class."

Another old friend from the food program which turned out to be favored with SYEP funds was B'nai Torah. On one B'nai Torah (JET Consortium) on-the-job training contract in 1974–75, almost half the employees placed were fired in less than thirty days, the supposed minimum for approval. However, the city renewed the contract the following year. This was only one of several million dollars worth of Comprehensive Employment Training Act contracts the city awarded to B'nai Torah or its affiliates during this period, and there is no reason to believe the others were run any better.

Other familiar organizations with SYEP contracts were the Crown Heights Community Corporation and the Hassidic Corporation for Urban Concerns (HCUC). We had researched both of these during the summer food program review, and both were important factors in an operation so complex that we had dubbed it the Pruzansky Empire. This empire was based in the Lubavitch Hassidic community in Crown Heights in Brooklyn, a center of the worldwide Lubavitch sect of the Hassidim, an Orthodox Jewish group. The members of the Pruzansky Empire were connected to each other through interlocking lawyers, directors, and employees and also informally through community ties.

The Pruzansky Empire did very, very well in obtaining government-funded programs. How well it ran the programs was the question that recurred.

I had first come into contact with the Pruzansky Empire back in 1975, when I was working in Elizabeth Holtzman's office. The rabbi who was chairman of HCUC had come to us with what sounded like a legitimate complaint. He said that the Department of Agriculture had rejected many of the distribution sites at which HCUC wanted to provide food for needy children in the summer food program. He explained that while in 1974 HCUC had been permitted to serve 200,000 lunches a day, for 1975 it had been cut back to 60,000 lunches a day. Although the rabbi admitted that the cut reflected new regulations that prohibited serving more than one meal per child per day, he asked me plaintively, "What am I to tell those seventy thousand kids?" He argued that sponsors with a "proven track record, like HCUC," should be permitted to retain a larger number of sites. However, when I followed up on this complaint by calling the Department of Agriculture, I was told that ongoing audits of the 1974 program indicated that HCUC had overbilled roughly $200,000 worth of reimbursements.

My impression of HCUC did not improve when, in 1976, we began our in-depth study of the food program. HCUC turned out to be the largest single sponsor of the city's 1976 food program. HCUC's vendor had been Pruzansky Brothers, Inc. Its principal, Joseph Pruzansky, was the father-in-law of the late Samuel Schrage, the behind-the-scenes linchpin of the Crown Heights group. Schrage was also a key political operative for the mayor in the Hassidic Jewish community. His name appeared nowhere in the records of the summer food program.

However, food program administrators, vendors, sponsor sources, and others reported his involvement as the principal of the 1976 Students for Torah International (disqualified from the 1977 program) and the representative and adviser of the B'nai Zaken sponsor in Chicago in 1975. B'nai Zaken, along with two other black and Jewish sponsors, engaged in bidding procedures in the 1976 New York program that were similar to those of the B'nai Torah group.

Schrage appears to have steered sponsors like Students for Torah International and B'nai Zaken to Crown Heights-related vendors, such as Community Development Services, run by former Pruzansky employees, or to Universal Caterers, run by a man who appears to have joined Pruzansky in a holding company. Schrage died in the fall of 1976.

In August 1976 the name Shragi Samuels was found on the summer food program payroll of the sponsor Chevra, an organization closely linked through a lawyer and three rabbis to the Crown Heights Jewish Community Council, the Community Training Organization, and Crown Heights Caterers, a vendor. Shragi Samuels was also found on the SYEP payroll of the Crown Heights Community Corporation. In the fall of 1976 one of the rabbis involved told me that Shragi Samuels was "a community woman who did some secretarial work for us." By the following spring one city agency had determined that Shragi Samuels was (1) male and (2) dead. The checks made out to Shragi Samuels were endorsed in different handwritings, sometimes to various officials of the organizations in question.

Even without the Schrage connection, it was obvious that HCUC was socially and politically part of the same organization that spawned the other Pruzansky groups mentioned. HCUC's chairman had been the representative of the Crown Heights Community Corporation on the city's Council Against Poverty. The National Committee for the Furtherance of Jewish Education, which included Pruzansky on the board of directors, was a sponsor in the food program. And the rabbi who ran the highly lucrative Crown Heights Caterers was paid as director of the Crown Heights Community Corporation's SYEP.

Despite all these intriguing linkages, during the food program scandal the Pruzansky group got off without even a press release from Congresswoman Holtzman. Compared to Pinter's

B'nai Torah group, which had been more or less sponsor-dominated, and the Velez group, which had been vendor-dominated, the Pruzansky group's structure had been a nightmare to untangle. It was an intricate collection of vendors and sponsors dominated by some of each. As I had written in a memo to Holtzman at the time, "If Pinter is *Portrait of the Artist*, and Velez is *Ulysses*, then Pruzansky is *Finnegans Wake*, and I can't manage it." While the Pruzansky Empire may have been guilty of more violations than Pinter's B'nai Torah, Pinter had provided the bidding information on which we had made our case against him. With Pruzansky, it had been difficult to see a pattern of bidding emerge primarily because those involved had been smart enough not to give much bidding information.

We did find a predated food program contract for HCUC (as we had for Pinter's B'nai Torah group), and on the basis of this discovery HCUC was denied the right to participate in the 1977 food program. Yet this was hardly satisfactory when we felt we were touching only the tip of the iceberg.

The Pruzansky group's summer food program contracts in New York City alone were worth many millions of dollars. In addition, we located valuable contracts for this group in Chicago, Los Angeles, and other cities. Having failed to make a thoroughgoing case ourselves, we hoped others might follow up. We therefore forwarded our material to the prosecutors' offices and some of it to the IRS as well. The district director of the IRS wrote to us on October 28, 1976:

> I assure you that we will carefully consider and evaluate the information and will take whatever action we deem appropriate considering all the facts and circumstances within the context of our resources and priorities. Disclosure statutes preclude me from giving you any additional information.

In other words: "We will do with your information exactly what we want, and we are not answerable to you." There was never any indication to the public or to us that the matter was pursued at all.

With this background, I was not surprised to see the Pruzansky group surface again in our new investigation of the youth employment program.

In order to qualify for job placement program funding, HCUC was supposed to have obtained commitments from employers to hire its program graduates, and such commitments were supposed to be in writing. But for a long time the comptroller's office was refused copies of the job placement forms. Finally, they arrived—all in the same handwriting.

The comptroller's office found that HCUC's $200,000 Comprehensive Employment and Training Act job placement contract for 1976–77 resulted in only about half the job placements it was contractually obligated to make. The other half of the youths had completed the program but had found work on their own. However, if more than 10 percent of a program's graduating jobholders had placed themselves, the program was not supposed to be approved. Nonetheless, the city recommended another $250,000 contract for HCUC's job placement program.

Meanwhile, the city had also approved another Pruzansky Empire member—the Crown Heights Community Corporation—for participation in SYEP, even though the closest its director came to describing the nature of the proposed job training was: "Probably all my sites will be work experience sites." In fact, this modest claim was an exaggeration. Despite loose monitoring, the city found that at 20 percent of the Crown Heights work sites there were either no Crown Heights workers or no work. Equally interesting was the nature of some sites where work did take place.

The Crown Heights Community Corporation, conveniently enough, sent some of its young SYEP participants for job placements at Chevra, a sponsor for the summer food program, supplied by Crown Heights Caterers. Here's how a Department of Agriculture health inspector described the caterer after a visit on August 11, 1976:

> No change from previous visit. Facility was too small for output (specifically the work area). Work area dirty and sloppy. Meat slicer did not appear to have been cleaned that day. Concrete floor was covered with oily film of unknown origin. Mr. Spritzer stated that the Health Depart-

ment had made an investigation, but he was unable to produce the report. He did have his permit to operate. *Facility should be closed* [emphasis in original].

Rabbi Samuel Spritzer was the proprietor of Crown Heights Caterers. He was also the supervisor for the Crown Heights Community Corporation's $790,000 SYEP funds. Thus, the federal government paid him for the food he produced and may have paid the salaries of the employees helping him produce it —a rather effective method of holding down costs and increasing profit margins.

In March 1977 Congresswoman Holtzman released a devastating study of SYEP, showing how sponsors like Bedford-Stuyvesant Youth-In-Action, the Crown Heights Community Corporation, and B'nai Torah failed to provide appropriate work experience and, indeed, could only have worsened any work habits their participants might have had.

Apparently not everyone agreed. The city's employment department, which ran the SYEP under government contract on behalf of the federal Department of Labor, gave Youth-In-Action 85 points out of a possible 100 for its SYEP—an unusually high grade—and approved Youth-In-Action for participation in the 1977 program on the basis of this 1976 record. Only the Crown Heights Community Corporation, of the many SYEP's that deserved to be, was actually disallowed from the 1977 program—and this was done by the Department of Labor, not by the city.

The city commissioner of employment during this period was Lucille Rose. Apparently on the basis of her handling of both the SYEP and the year-round Comprehensive Employment and Training Act programs, the mayor elevated her to deputy mayor. Her successor not surprisingly continued the same policies in 1977. Rose's rapid political ascent is understandable given the power groups she catered to: Youth-In-Action, which at one time or another counted on its board most of the political leadership of the Bedford-Stuyvesant neighborhood; B'nai Torah, with its national-level connections; and HCUC, with its power base in the disciplined voters of the Lubavitch Hassidic election districts of the Crown Heights neighborhood. With such allies, Rose became in her own right a powerful political force.

For example, in May 1977 *New York Times* reporter Charles Kaiser reported that the mayor was still supporting a $1 million job training program contract for B'nai Torah, after all the summer food program revelations and the job program revelations. Kaiser also noted that the comptroller's office had prepared a highly negative audit on Comprehensive Employment and Training Act contractors, including B'nai Torah, in November 1976. Had such an audit been released, on top of Holtzman's disclosures regarding B'nai Torah (see Chapter 1), it would have been much more difficult for the mayor to support B'nai Torah's contract award. However, Kaiser noted that the report, without having been made public, "had been vigorously denounced by Mrs. Rose" and thus had never been released. Why Rose, a mayoral appointee, got an advance peek at a report by the comptroller—whose most important job it is to provide a check or a balance to the mayor—is an open question. (A later attempt by the U.S. Department of Labor to make Rose its regional administrator was dropped after Kaiser's published reminder of her involvement with B'nai Torah.)

Kaiser, in a subtle way, was demonstrating that the comptroller, despite a carefully cultivated image as reformer, was trying to remain at peace with Rose's political forces. Later (January 31, 1978), less subtly, Kaiser would write in the *Times* of an advance briefing given by the comptroller's office to an official of B'nai Torah on an upcoming audit. Such a briefing must have warned B'nai Torah to cover up anything that might look suspicious or prove embarrassing.

Meanwhile, in the next day's *Times* (May 27, 1977), Kaiser reported that the Board of Estimate had postponed action on the contract request for B'nai Torah. Although Kaiser didn't say so, this was obviously in response to his article the day before. Kaiser did report that the board had *approved* a $500,000 contract for a Pruzansky group closely connected with another sponsor that had been criticized in the comptroller's November audit. By this time the comptroller's office was getting the message, and Kaiser was able to report that the seven-month-old audit would be released the following week.

But in June 1977 the Department of Labor, which had

pledged to investigate the 1976 SYEP sponsors, urged the city's Board of Estimate to continue funding B'nai Torah. This incredible move, while B'nai Torah was still under investigation by the departments of Justice and Agriculture as well as Labor, was just the excuse the mayor needed to renew his support for B'nai Torah. On June 23 the board voted B'nai Torah the $1 million job training contract.

The following January the affidavit of Stephen Elko, Congressman Daniel Flood's aide, became public. Elko revealed that B'nai Torah's Rabbi Lieb Pinter had bribed Flood to intervene with the Labor Department to get job training contracts. Pinter later admitted the bribery. The Labor Department's protective attitude toward B'nai Torah is understandable since Flood's subcommittee in Congress had jurisdiction over the Labor Department's budget (as well as over the summer food program budget, although it is under the Agriculture Department).

Not until April 13, 1978, after several of Pinter's assistants had already been convicted, did the Secretary of Labor admit "at this late date" that his department's "investigation" had been incomplete.

The bribe from B'nai Torah to Congressman Flood hints at possible relationships on other government levels and between other participants. No other evidence of bribes by other large poverty groups or of wrongdoing by members of the mayor's administration has surfaced. But any attempt to explain the persistent protection of these groups must at least consider the possibility that the Pinter bribe to Flood was unique only in that Pinter got caught, that unethical and often illegal political and financial transactions underlay the whole of the poverty program mess.

In January 1978 the city had a new mayor. He was alerted that HCUC, with one of the worst job training performance records in the city for the millions of dollars it had already received, was about to get another quarter of a million dollars from the Board of Estimate with the city employment department's support. The request to have this budget appropriation added to the calendar was denied.

On April 19, 1978, the new administration's employment

commissioner initiated a thorough audit of one of the most powerful components of the Pruzansky group, the National Committee for the Furtherance of Jewish Education, after forcing the director to remove his son and daughter from the public payroll in his employment program. Previous officials of the employment department had allowed this, even though nepotism is specifically and absolutely proscribed by Comprehensive Employment Training Act regulations. On July 15, 1978, the group's $2.5 million jobs program contract was terminated.

On June 23 contracts for Bedford-Stuyvesant Youth-In-Action and the Crown Heights Community Corporation were terminated.

To the outraged cries of community leaders who had been running the SYEP projects, the new employment commissioner required that the summer jobs be awarded by lottery, thus taking these job distribution powers out of their hands. On July 10, 1979, the director of the city's SYEP said, "For the first time in history, we have the program under control." Confounding the community leaders' accusations that the reform movement had been motivated by racism, 92 percent of the participants in the postlottery program were from minorities, as compared with 75 percent before the lottery.

Charges of corruption in federally funded employment programs were hardly unique to New York. On February 1, 1979, President Carter's domestic policy chief, Stuart Eizenstat, announced a "broad program of reforms" designed to correct the fraud and abuse which the federal government belatedly admitted were plaguing the Comprehensive Employment Training Act programs. Eizenstat revealed that over the previous thirteen months the Labor Department's new inspector general's office had contributed to sixty-seven indictments and twenty-four convictions for fraud.

8

The $500-a-Month Slum

No MATTER HOW HARD you try to husband your resources for reform cases in which you have a good chance of success, a few failures are inevitable. This is especially frustrating when you have made a good start and feel you may be on to something but then are unable to marshal evidence.

I became involved in such a case in 1978 after meeting Howard, a retired postal worker. For a decade Howard had directed his energies toward improving his neighborhood. That was the South Bronx, a predominantly Hispanic, poor, and very tough area. Howard exuded warmth and affection, one reason this small middle-aged black man had become such a beloved neighborhood leader. He was a curious man, though, and our feelings about him became fond exasperation somehow mixed with admiration. He was energetic, persistent to the point of mania, idealistic, honest, and careless of facts. In many ways he was an excellent source, but he almost drove us crazy.

Howard was angry about conditions in his housing project, which had been built under Section Eight. In 1974 Congress had passed Section Eight of the national housing act to provide rent supplements for poverty-stricken families living in designated new and rehabilitated housing. Its apparent intent was to enable landlords to supply decent housing to impoverished tenants. I. D. Robbins, writing in the New York *Daily News* on July 17, 1979, estimated that about $290 million in such rent supplements were provided to about 50,000 households in New York City.

In practice, the law was a boon to landlords. They used Section Eight as part of a lucrative and perfectly legal tax shelter scheme. Subsidies, like the Section Eight Housing Assistance Payments (HAP), are not considered income for tax purposes. Thus, for tax purposes the landlords "lose" money on these rent-assisted buildings. They usually put 10 percent down and get government-guaranteed mortgages for the rest of the purchase price, but they take paper losses as if they had used only their own money. They don't really lose money because they get the HAP subsidies.

In the case of the project where Howard lived, investors put up about $6 million in cash in exchange for tax write-offs of about $24 million.

Against tough competition from sources for other investigations, Howard's presentation was by far the most convoluted, confusing, and disorganized. The subjects of his charges ranged from the Mafia to the White House. The tales of tenant woe he told ranged from failure to provide common-use washing machines to physical crimes perpetrated against tenants by the developments' security guards.

What proved most amazing was that so much of what Howard had to say we later discovered was true.

I am simplifying the story somewhat. Howard actually told us about *two* projects, one with eight buildings and the other with at least twenty buildings. The two had different owners, operated under different federal programs, and had different problems. Their component buildings, however, were physically intermingled, and Howard made little effort to clarify for us the distinctions between them in his story. This probably confused us sufficiently to delay our comprehension for several months.

Howard told us that the buildings in the larger project were rehabilitated in the early 1970's with cheap, used, and defective materials and that as a result, walls and ceilings were constantly developing holes and leaks. He told us that the developer also managed the project through a wholly owned subsidiary. He told us that the management firm provided virtually no services beyond collecting rent; tenants froze in the winter; ceilings leaked; icicles grew in apartments; and hallway lights stayed out, often with hanging exposed wiring, creating darkened traps where muggers surprised their victims. He told us that the underpaid, unqualified security guards hired by the management were a significant source of the crime problem themselves, raping and burglarizing the tenants at will. He told us of years of unanswered complaints to the federal Department of Housing and Urban Development (HUD), which was supposedly responsible for monitoring the project to ensure compliance with HUD's Section Eight funding regulations. He told us that the regulations requiring the provision of decent, safe, and sanitary housing were regularly violated, yet the developer had received millions of dollars of HAP payments since 1974.

Most interesting of all, he told us that he had written to Congressman Thomas Ashley, chairman of the House Banking Subcommittee on Housing and County Development, reporting these problems. With his letter Howard sent a petition from the tenants. Ashley contacted HUD, which sent an investigator. The investigator, said Howard, gradually realized that an enormous political scandal must have been behind HUD's refusal to provide effective monitoring of the developer over the years. But just about the time the HUD investigator reached this conclusion, he was pulled off the case, transferred to Texas, and eventually fired. A muffled phone call from the investigator in Washington relating these developments was the last Howard had heard of him, and he had been unable to find the investigator since.

Our investigation was not entirely a pioneering effort. Robert Sheer of the Los Angeles *Times* had visited the projects in June 1978 to research a series he was doing on urban decay in the United States. On August 7, 1978, his article appeared on page 1 of the L.A. *Times,* and it provided a good sense of the project story's political context.

At the time of Sheer's story the developer's chief New York official was president of the National Rehabilitated Housing Association. The Washington law firm representing the association included the man who had headed President Carter's transition team on housing. Sheer quoted the president of the National Rehabilitated Housing Association as saying that when he had sent a note to then Treasury Secretary Michael Blumenthal and to the White House asking them to correct the "oversight" that omitted the tax shelter for housing rehabilitation from the administration's tax reform package, it was "corrected" immediately. Sheer's description of this "good rapport with the Carter Administration" gave us an inkling we might be dealing with a large web of important connections.

This was tantalizing but elusive. We still didn't know where the federal money was going—since it was not going to the maintenance of the buildings—or whether Howard's mysterious story of the missing HUD investigator was true.

We decided that what we already knew was enough for a first cut at the issue. We visited the project and saw the apartments Howard described—without heat, with huge chunks of plaster falling from walls and ceilings, darkened hallways, broken doors, and intercoms—for which the developer was receiving up to $535 a month in rent. On February 11 we charged in a press release that the federal government was spending millions to house Bronx families in rat-infested tenements. We demanded of HUD: "Take Action to Clean Up 1,312-Unit Project Known as New York City's 'Black Hole of Calcutta'!"

Sadly, New Yorkers are all too accustomed to stories of suffering tenants. The most likely explanation of why this story received any coverage at all was that our press expert had dubbed the project New York City's "Black Hole of Calcutta." It had been known as such, until our press release, only to us.

The next step was as outrageous as it was frustrating. Permission to review key documents concerning the project was denied to our subcommittee staffer at a meeting with high-level New York regional HUD officials on February 28, 1979. Not until we sent a Freedom of Information Act request to then HUD Secretary Patricia Harris were the files made available to us. Even then they were presented in a snow-job-style meeting that the New York regional HUD staff held with us, obviously on orders from Washington.

We assigned a staffer to the project virtually full time, and he did a prodigious amount of digging through and analyzing mountains of files. His ten years in the academic world and his earlier years as a disillusioned marine in Vietnam gave him the right combination of persistence, thoroughness, and skepticism needed for the job. He reported that the developer had received about $1 million since 1976 for apartments which did not meet the "minimum physical criteria for safer, sanitary, and decent" living conditions required by HUD regulations for eligibility for HAP. Another $1.5 million were received for tenants without evidence of income eligibility, for apartments that were actually vacant for which the developer claimed occupancy, and for other deceptions.

Of course, HUD's New York regional office had made virtually no effort to avoid being deceived in this manner, although, on the basis of tenant complaints, officials had every reason to suspect such deception. HUD had simply turned a deaf ear.

Our investigation, however, did not go much further. After learning that the missing HUD investigator had been active in Carter's presidential campaign, I called the White House to see if it could find him. It could, and it did.

I reached the investigator at the home telephone number provided by the White House. He corroborated Howard's story that an HUD official had ordered him to "stay away" from the investigation without explaining why. The investigator had been reassigned shortly thereafter and had later left HUD.

This corroboration was interesting because Congressman Ashley had written Howard that congressional hearings were "inappropriate" because HUD was going to investigate the matter itself. If HUD had promised to investigate the projects and then told its investigator to stay away from the case, its actions were peculiar indeed.

We dug around some more and found connections between certain HUD officials and some New York developers who operated under Section Eight. This suggested guilt by association. Despite an additional year of continued effort, we were unable to trace these connections to any evidence of criminal wrongdoing.

So here was a case where we seemed to have a good source

and where our early inquiries turned up some tantalizing suspicions. Failing to convert these suspicions into evidence against either the regional HUD office or the department in Washington was frustrating. Most aggravating of all was not knowing whether we had been on the wrong track or whether evidence had escaped us.

9

The Secret Good Government Mafia and the War Against the Poverty Program Empires

THIS CHAPTER TELLS a story that is more complicated than most in this book. Unlike most of the others, it does not tell of a single investigation of a single scandal and consequent reform. Instead, it tells of the network of formal, informal, and indeed secret relationships among several investigators and their war against several scandals in the federal poverty programs that turned out to be connected. For the most part, the investigators won the war, but it is hard to show precise cause-and-effect relationships. Rather, the cumulative effect of investigations by a congresswoman and her assistant, a political candidate, a mayoral aide, reporters, a federal prosecutor, myself, and others helped undo one mayoral administration and resulted in massive reforms of the poverty programs under a new mayor. Also, our efforts helped awaken the highest levels of the federal government to a need for a change in their attitude toward administering the poverty programs after a period of excessive tolerance or worse.

The most persistent subjects of exposé in 1976 and 1977 were the programs originally designed to provide help to the poor. Welfare fraud had long been a reliable standby for newspapers. But the new focus was different. Community development, job training, nutritional assistance, drug abuse treatment—these were now the programs subject to charges of major abuse and corruption. To the newspaper reader, the links among these scandals may not have been apparent. Indeed, at the beginning they were not apparent to us, the reformers, who were the sources of the news. But eventually a single pattern came into focus.

By 1966 Lyndon Johnson's War Against Poverty had been emasculated, some say by the diversion of funds and effort to the war in Vietnam, some say by the political efforts of existing power structures, which feared that the mandated "maximum feasible participation of the poor" in the poverty programs would create rival power structures. But individual poverty programs did continue to receive funding, even through the further ravages of the Nixon and Ford administrations.

The urban riots of the late 1960's influenced policies and perceptions of the poverty programs. In many cities across the country it appeared that poverty programs funds were used in an unsophisticated way to prevent riots. That is, political aides were said to have gone systematically to militant community spokespersons, seen as potential leaders of riots, and offered them "programs" to keep them quiet. These programs were understood by both sides to be little more than euphemisms for bribes. The recipients were not expected to perform actual services, such as job training or drug abuse treatment.

There were exceptions, of course; community groups and leaders of integrity and intelligence did organize some meaningful efforts. But the overall picture was bleak. I was among those who believed that something was radically wrong with New York City's Council Against Poverty, the central policy-making and money-distributing "board of directors" of the city's poverty programs. Money supposedly distributed on the basis of need was actually allocated to "community corporations" representing the twenty-six poverty areas of the city by a bargaining process fundamentally composed of kickbacks, violence, and threats of violence.

The corporations were supposed to represent the below-poverty-line voters in the neighborhoods that elected their directors. The corporations were supposed to act as vehicles for distributing antipoverty moneys to worthy programs in those neighborhoods. In reality, most of the corporations were quickly taken over by political hacks, old or new, and rarely served any interests but their own.

Although all this was known in a vague way in political circles, it took years to build enough legally supportable evidence to crush the community corporations. Throughout this process the city was remarkably slow to acknowledge what was going on. Not until late 1977—long after most of the important work in exposing the corruption had been accomplished—did an official audit by the city comptroller finally state that the allocation of poverty program money by the Council Against Poverty "is not and never had been based on need."

The first major breakthrough in reforming the poverty programs in New York was the exposure of the summer food program scandal (see Chapter 1). This operation had first been questioned in 1975 by Elizabeth "Ibby" Lang, a talented and idealistic young lawyer working for Congresswoman Elizaabeth Holtzman, but serious investigation had not begun until 1976. As I was also working for Holtzman, Lang and I shared around-the-clock marathon sessions. These long hours over a period of months, "fighting the good fight" against waste and corruption, seemingly just us against the wealthy, powerful establishment, built a relationship that transcended our formal roles as fellow employees.

Every major "poverty pimp," or exploiter of poverty programs, seemed to have found his way into this particular program. Our review of the participants gave us a good basic understanding of the structure of poverty program corruption in the city. Out of that understanding came the eventual exposure and reform of the "empires," the organizations and their leadership, that dominated the poverty programs, job training programs, and community corporations in New York.

Naturally, when I left Holtzman's office in 1977 to join the Subcommittee on City Management, I continued to share information and exchange ideas with Lang. Thus, when I began to explore drug treatment programs (see Chapters 4, 5, and 6) and again stumbled on Bedford-Stuyvesant Youth-In-Action, which Lang and I had investigated in connection with the summer food program, I conferred with her.

At that time Ibby Lang was looking into the Summer Youth Employment Program (SYEP), funded by the Comprehensive Employment Training Act, for Holtzman. During this inquiry she had found Youth-In-Action in the most egregious violations of SYEP rules (see Chapter 7).

Lang was also in regular communication with Gary Deane of the city comptroller's staff, who was investigating the year-round programs funded by the same Comprehensive Employment Training Act. Deane was also discovering that these programs were dominated by the suspects we had turned up in the food program.

Like Lang and me, Gary Deane was a reformer. Out of an ascetic Roman Catholic background, he had considered the priesthood but became involved, instead, in civil rights, gay rights, labor organizing, and other causes. In 1976 he was the comptroller's representative on the Board of Estimate on poverty program issues, with power to approve funding on the comptroller's behalf. Part of his responsibility was to determine whether a sponsor's past performance justified additional funding. In this extremely difficult, important, and even dangerous work he was frustrated by lack of support or interest from his superiors. As a result, he, too, developed a close relationship with the sympathetic Ibby Lang.

Once Lang, Deane, and I had become informally involved in the Summer Youth Employment Program (see Chapter 7), we formed a clear picture of four major "empires" that were exploiting poverty programs in the city:

B'nai Torah, a flagrant violator in the food program, was also involved in youth employment scandals.

Bedford-Stuyvesant Youth-In-Action had similarly first come to our attention during the food program investigation. As we began to see the scope and scale of Youth-In-Action's operations in drug programs and employment programs, we realized that this group in and of itself constituted a poverty program empire.

The Pruzansky group, which included the Hassidic Corporation for Urban Concerns and the Crown Heights Community Corporation, had also turned out to be adept at collecting poverty funds under the same three programs without delivering the promised services.

In addition, there was a complex empire we first called the Macaluso group because our initial investigation had centered on the activities of Joseph Macaluso and his son. Later, however, we realized that the Macaluso operations were only part of a wider complex of relationships that were linked through City Councilman Ramon Velez. We therefore renamed this group the Velez Empire.

In our 1976 food program inquiry the Macaluso-Velez group had had the distinction of providing the least wholesome meals prepared under the most repulsive conditions. The group was a loosely organized collection of thirty-seven sponsors apparently linked through six vendors. The largest vendor was Road Chef International, which we nicknamed Roach Chef or Rodent Chef. Run by Joseph Macaluso, Road Chef was the subject of fourteen separate city, state, and federal health inspections all citing violations, including filth, unsanitary procedures, and unpalatable and nutritionally unacceptable food. Its inspections the previous summer had yielded similar results. Yet eleven sponsors selected this vendor in 1976, supposedly as a result of a competitive bidding process, although the bids were all at or *above* the maximum permitted price. Five of the sponsors chose it over lower bidders, citing the "high quality" of its food.

Somehow, before receiving any contract, Road Chef—which could hardly have counted on getting business solely on the basis of its past performance—had enough confidence or foresight to order 200,000 meat turnovers per week in advance from its supplier. *All* of Road Chef's sponsors were found to have violated competitive bidding requirements. Although supposedly independent of one another, seven sponsors submitted to the government documents that contained identical wording. Most of these sponsors were community corporations, the neighborhood antipoverty organizations, and most of them had connections of some kind with City Councilman Ramon Velez.

Joseph Macaluso, Sr., was president of Four Star School Feeding Corporation. With a health record similar to that of Road Chef's, Four Star had contracts with eight sponsors. One of these, the Red Hook Christian Methodist Episcopal Church, the records of which had been "stolen" from the Brooklyn food program office, was an entirely fictitious organization. It established its tax-exempt eligibility by using a letter purportedly signed by Bishop Henry Bunton of the Christian Methodist Episcopal Church in Washington stating that Red Hook was an affiliate church. Bishop Bunton told me, "I never wrote any such letter; it is a forgery." In fact, there was no church at the address Red Hook gave the government. Rather, the building there was owned by Four Star, Red Hook's vendor. Four Star's other contracts were equally questionable. One sponsor, choosing Four Star over a lower bidder, explained that its previous record was "especially appealing." One wonders if the sponsor was referring to Four Star's 1975 health inspection citations for "possible rodent harborage" and "garbage and debris."

Researching the Macaluso group gave us a quick introduction to a large cast of characters centered on City Councilmen Ramon Velez and Samuel Wright, who would appear in questionable roles in subsequent investigations of different poverty programs. We turned over all our material on this group to federal prosecutors, just as we had turned over the Lieb Pinter and B'nai Torah material. On March 13, 1979, Lynette Lewis and the Reverend Charles Hall, of the Red Hook Methodist Episcopal Church, and Joseph Macaluso, Sr., and Edgar Lunford, of the Four Star School Feeding Corporation, were indicted for fraud in connection with the 1976 summer lunch program.

Interestingly, Arthur Browne, writing for the New York *Daily News* in November 1976, one month after our Macaluso exposé, noted that Road Chef had made a $1 million profit in the nine-week lunch program. Browne also reported that Road Chef's president, Salvatore Fariello, had been charged in 1969 as the "kingpin" in a terror campaign against a rival ice cream company, convicted of third-degree larceny, and received probation and a $1,000 fine. In 1970 he had pleaded guilty to another count of grand larceny and again got probation.

One of the pillars of the Velez Empire was the SERA drug program (see Chapter 4) under the immediate supervision of Roberto Munoz. Munoz was the former executive director of the Hunts Point Community Corporation under the leadership of then City Councilman Ramon Velez. Munoz was also both a board member of Velez's Puerto Rican Community Development Project (PRCDP) and a subcontractor of PRCDP, under the name of the Puerto Rican Civil Rights League. In normal business and government affairs, of course, such dual roles are considered questionable.

Munoz's son-in-law was the mayor's commissioner of the Community Development Administration. As such, he was theoretically responsible for evaluating antipoverty programs, including those of Munoz and Velez. The son-in-law was also on the committee responsible for directing the elections to the community corporation boards, again including those controlled by Velez.

One of the methods by which Velez retained control of the various components of his empire was to make employees of one of his operations directors of others. Thus, the treasurer of the Hunts Point Community Corporation was the executive director of PRCDP. The director of the Hunts Point Community Corporation was the treasurer of PRCDP. The chairman of PRCDP was an employee of another Velez-controlled enterprise. So each member of the supposed directorate of a Velez organization had to rely for his salary on another Velez-controlled organization. But PRCDP was the jewel in the crown. In May 1977 Murray Kempton of the New York *Post* had written that the Puerto Rican Community Development Project had collected nearly "$3 million a year in federal grants and is thus to the Velez poverty empire what Byzantium was to Rome in the East."

Gary Deane, during his time in the comptroller's office, had found that Velez's PRCDP placed $30,000 in program funds in two secret personal bank accounts for the personal use of certain employees who were close to Velez. In reviewing PRCDP documents submitted to the Board of Estimate in support of applications for funding, Deane had seen some entries that he thought raised questions. His inquiries led him to a few frightened but honest Velez employees, who met with him in secret at night in South Bronx coffee shops, supplied him with copies of Velez's records of those with personal access to the bank accounts, and warned him in Spanish of the danger to all their lives.

Although Deane reported the PRCDP slush fund to the comptroller, this information was not made public until Deane released it on October 31, 1977, while running for office himself, at which time the comptroller's office released it simultaneously. By that time Velez had lost his city councilman's primary, and Kempton wrote, noting Velez's legal battle to reverse the results of that race, "Velez lost the Democratic primary last summer; and, unless the courts abandon all reason, we seem likely to be bereft of his legislative wisdom in the future. He remains, however, in being and in mischief, as proprietor of poverty programs with a budget of nearly $4.5 million. . . ."

Two months later the deputy mayor supported PRCDP's half-million-dollar Comprehensive Employment Training Act program contract request before the Board of Estimate. (By June 1978 three PRCDP officials had been indicted on the basis of the Manhattan DA's investigation of Deane's charges.)

In October 1977 I was asked to chair a secret Poverty Programs Committee of the Edward Koch Mayoral Transition Team. By then Koch was the Democratic nominee for mayor, and his election seemed likely. I was told that the Koch administration wanted the information in order to know "who the crooks were" in the poverty programs and what could be done to make the programs work better. Knowing that there were no better sources than Lang and Deane, I asked them to serve with me on the committee. As protection against libel suits, our committee and its report were to remain secret from all except certain members of the Koch administration and the Manhattan district attorney's office.

My friends in the United States attorney's office used to say, "You catch only the dumb crooks, not the smart ones." Many times in our investigations, when our evidence was inadequate for criminal charges or even for a press release, we *knew* our targets were guilty. Sometimes our sources were utterly trustworthy and had personal knowledge of malfeasance on which, for one reason or another, they could not give public testimony. Often circumstances that we understood, because of our long involvement in a case, demonstrated guilt to us in a way that we could not really explain to others. After weeks or months of investigation it seemed there was nothing we could do to prevent culprits from getting off scot-free, possibly with heaps of ill-gotten gains.

So the offer to tell the next mayor who the crooks were, without the need for evidence that would hold up in a court of law, was irresistible. In retrospect, I have some qualms about having been party to what was intended as, and indeed seems for a while to have been used as, a secret blacklist. It is hard to see how it fits into my general ethical scheme of reform, which stresses exercise of First Amendment rights. But at the time, in the excitement of an apparently golden opportunity for massive, sweeping reform of the poverty programs, these considerations did not occur to me.

During two incredibly hectic weeks in October 1977 Deane, Lang, and I engaged in our normal pursuits during the day and spent the nights writing our secret fifty-page report. For Deane, who was running for councilman-at-large, this meant an extra sacrifice during the tense and difficult last weeks of his campaign. He lost his race.

The report described the workings of the four "empires": Youth-In-Action, B'nai Torah, Pruzansky, and the Velez group. It described structural problems in the Comprehensive Employment Training Act programs, community corporations, and antipoverty programs, and it made recommendations to the administration for reform.

Although we had evidence of the bribing of public officials only on the part of B'nai Torah, we noted that it was by no means the only organization whose history in the poverty programs indicated otherwise inexplicable degrees of official tolerance.

One of the strongest warnings Deane, Lang, and I issued in our secret committee report was the need to postpone antipoverty corporation elections that had been scheduled for February 28, 1979, in order to give the new administration time to take the elections process out of the hands of the insiders who controlled it.

On January 1, 1978, in the only substantive section of his

inaugural address, Mayor Koch said, "In the past, programs that were meant to help the needy ended up as bonanzas for the greedy. . . . And now our city treasury is nearly empty, and it must be wisely managed."

Less than two weeks later I was asked for another confidential memorandum, this time on several community groups who were applying for approval as constituents of the community corporations to be newly organized. Again, I stressed the need for postponement of the community corporation elections.

On January 16 Koch asked the Community Services Administration, the federal antipoverty organization in charge, to delay the elections. A six-month delay was granted on February 8.

The New York *Post*, under a huge front-page headline reading "Crackdown on Poverty Rackets," on January 19 reported Koch's statement that "I do not intend to allow any anti-poverty funds to be administered by any board that has a miscreant whose crime is job-related." Groups affected would include Velez's Hunts Point Community Corporation and Councilman Sam Wright's Brownsville Community Development Corporation. Also, a proposed grant to the Fort Greene Community Corporation was immediately withdrawn because of the presence of David Billings on its board. Billings had been convicted in 1976 of misuse of federal job funds and had been chairman of the Council Against Poverty during the period when I found it to have been characterized by kickbacks and violence.

On April 19 an audit was begun of the National Committee for the Furtherance of Jewish Education, a powerful component of the Pruzansky group, and three months later its $2.5 million jobs program contract was terminated.

On April 28 the city terminated its contract with Velez's Hunts Point Community Corporation because of evidence of "possible fiscal fraud." On May 18 the Morrisania Community Corporation's contract was canceled for "a consistent, interrelated pattern of mismanagement and abuse." On June 23 contracts of Youth-In-Action, the Crown Heights Community Corporation, the East New York Community Corporation, the East Harlem Community Corporation, and the Lower East

Side Community Corporation were terminated. The *Times* noted the next day that "the most recent audit of Youth-In-Action indicated that more than 95% of the funds for which the corporation is responsible 'are managed with accounting systems deemed inadequate to safeguard the resources.'" Youth-In-Action had been stealing millions for at least five years.

Our secret committee had recommended the dissolution of the community corporations. We wrote, in our report to the mayor:

> The community corporations have neither facilitated delivery of services to the poor nor acted as effective advocates for the poor. Over and over again the complaint is heard from the neighborhoods—"we never see any of that money, it all goes into the pockets of the Board members and community corporation employees."
>
> The community corporations are a symbol of rip-off. They have never worked. . . .

On February 16, 1979, the community corporations went out of existence. The federal Community Services Administration accepted the mayor's restructuring plan, which replaced the corporations with area policy boards, roughly conforming to our committee's recommendations. The new plan empowered the city to keep tight fiscal controls on any funded groups.

Thus, our report, though it remained secret, had had considerable impact. In a memorandum to his editors at the *Times*, Kaiser had written at one point, without knowing of the committee, that Deane, Lang, and I were a sort of "secret good government mafia" operating behind the scenes and sharing information in an informal and unofficial bridge of three levels of government—Lang a federal congressional employee, I counsel to a subcommittee of the state legislature, and Deane (by that time) a city government employee on the staff of the City Council president. Kaiser had regularly called on each of us for source material and quickly realized that we had been working together on many projects.

The committee was the only formal joint effort among

Lang, Deane, and me, but it grew out of a network of informal relationships that preceded and succeeded the existence of the committee itself. In fact, the good government Mafia comprised many more people than our committee's tiny nuclear family. In any field, informal relationships are frequently as important as or more important than official relationships, and the field of investigative reform of government is no different.

Kaiser himself, who had covered the Board of Estimate politics of poverty program funding, along with fellow journalists on other city newspapers, had contributed to the defeat of the old administration. Lang had developed good relations with the U.S. attorney's office during the prosecution of Rabbi Pinter and through other associations. Lang and I had friends in the mayor's staff, too. Only through such widening circles of contact, with feedback from many different concerned sources, can large corrupt power blocs be battled successfully.

Only time will tell exactly how extensive are the improvements in the poverty programs in New York. Clearly, eternal vigilance is the price not only of liberty but also of honesty. In the fall of 1979 Ramon Velez, although not returned to public office, was still in control of antipoverty organizations receiving millions of dollars in city and federal funds. Along with his wife and employees, he had been appointed to a Bronx community planning board by the Bronx borough president. Gary Deane was still on his trail, helping bring these matters to public notice. It is indisputable, however, that to a significant extent our efforts to reform the poverty programs worked—at least for a while.

10

Missing Bodies

In the summer of 1977 an otherwise occupied friendly New York *Post* reporter suggested to the Subcommittee on City Management that we "look into the fire department situation." Usually we would have ignored a tip so vague. But this one was different. First, it came from a highly respected and valued friend. Secondly, it came with names of people to call, including a fire engine dispatcher and a high-ranking fire officers' union official.

The contacts gave us an alarming and intriguing story: The department's top brass was underreporting fire fatalities in an effort to make the mayor's budget cuts in the department look acceptable. The fire commissioner, proud of his management capabilities, was trying to show what a good job he could do despite crippling cutbacks. Our sources referred us to Rodrick and Deborah Wallace. This husband-and-wife research team made a hobby of studying municipal fires and crusading to uncover the truth through statistical analyses.

The Wallaces showed us their analyses of officially reported fire fatalities statistics from 1972 to 1976. The figures after 1972 showed an almost perfect (0.99) correlation between an increase in the number of structural fires and a *decrease* in the number of people dying in fires. This statistical relationship seemed extremely unlikely. The more fires, the fewer deaths? Conceivably the two variables might lack a strong positive correlation; arson can increase at the same time that new technology allows fire fighters to get to fires

113

faster, thus preventing deaths. But a strong negative correlation, showing fewer deaths in an almost exact relationship with more fires, was hard to believe.

Indeed, the department did seem to reach fires faster. A second statistic the Wallaces showed us indicated that engine response time had dropped between 1972 and 1975—by exactly the same decrease each year. This was even harder to believe since the department had been enlarging the geographical area that each of its units had to cover during those years.

Here the department could argue that it was improving its positioning of units so effectively that even with larger areas to cover, average response time was dropping. Unfortunately for the department's case, the figures it reported for "work time" (the time fire officers are at the scenes of fires) were greater than its figures for "operational time" (the total time from receipt of alarm to return to quarters). This intriguing discrepancy cast doubt on any statistical presentation the department was attempting to make.

But we knew that a statistical case against the fire department would not be enough. The department, because of its superior expertise about its own operations, could talk around a statistical attack, even a correct one. To make the case definitive and to get the headlines we would need to generate pressure for change, we had to find the missing bodies.

In this effort, our contacts in the fire unions were crucial. First, Edward Jennings, president of the Uniformed Fire Officers Association, established a framework for us by recounting a session with the fire commissioner in which Jennings challenged the official 1976 figure of 236 fatalities. The fire commissioner first conceded that 8 deaths were not included and finally admitted that 46 deaths had been left out—for a real total of 282.

But the clincher was the deaths themselves—the specifics. Union officials pointed us to a fire in Staten Island which killed two children, as reported by the *Daily News*. The fire department reported only one. Of ten people known to be in a department store when it caught fire and still missing weeks afterward, only four were on the department's fatality list. A thirty-six-year-old male, a twenty-six-year-old male, two teenagers, and a seventy-six-year-old woman were also somehow left out.

We learned that under the previous commissioner's tenure such errors had virtually never been made. The body count was of grave importance, and a fire officer who failed to report a fatality found himself in serious trouble. It was clear, given the scale of the omissions (forty-six by the commissioner's own admission to Jennings), that this was no mere statistical discrepancy.

The Wallaces concluded, strictly on the basis of their statistical studies, that a policy decision had been made by the department to report a decrease in fire deaths, starting in 1974. It looked as if the policy were designed to persuade the public that the city could cut fire protection and not lose lives as a result.

Had the official 1976 fatality figure of 236 deaths been accurate, it would have reflected a 3 percent decline in fatalities from the 1975 figure of 244 deaths. The commissioner's initial "correction" to 244 deaths would have made the figures even. But the final "corrected" figure of 282 deaths reflected more than a 15 percent increase over 1975. The department had known about most of the additional deaths in January 1977; one question it never answered was why it had not included those deaths on the January list but instead had waited until March to make the correction.

The first page of the New York *Post* on Monday, September 26, 1977, read "Coverup Rap in Fatal Fires Here." The television stations showed Assemblyman Schumer standing in front of what we had billed in our advisory as an "eerie burnt-out scene of an unrecorded fire death"—the seventy-six-year-old woman.

We had not counted on the press relations skill and connections of the fire department.

Four hours after our press conference the department held its own. Cass Vanzi of the *Daily News*, a regular fire story reporter, covered the rebuttal press conference, although she had not come to ours. The headline of the only *Daily News* story about either press conference read "No Coverup, Just a Mix-up." It continued, "Acting Fire Commissioner Stephen Murphy said at Fire Headquarters, 110 Church Street, that the department was not involved in any coverup of fire deaths and would be pleased to make a record available to Schumer or any other elected official." Murphy explained that the official figure had been raised to 282—without, of course, mentioning Jennings's challenge, which had got it raised—and said that the discrepancy had been due to poor communication with the medical examiner's office.

This entirely blunted the focus of the story: The "discrepancy" had been hidden long enough to disguise from the public the literally fatal impact of budget cuts. Since the media did not pick up the issue of engine response time, which was not so sensational as deaths, Murphy was not forced to explain why a second department statistic also appeared to be faked.

On October 8 we refuted the fire department's response, disclosing 8 more deaths still not listed in the "final" figure of 282. We pointed out that despite its publicly asserted willingness to make records available, the department would not give us access to lists of fatalities prior to 1976 or to fire marshal reports from any time period. But we learned that the media do not like to cover a rebuttal of a rebuttal. We got no coverage.

Much later the New York *Post* did an exposé of the fire commissioner's personal improprieties, including the flashing red light he had had installed, at city expense, on the car of Dick Oliver, city editor of the *Daily News*. But our exposé was the first bad press the commissioner had ever gotten. It broke the dam and made it easier for the new mayor not to reappoint him.

Much more important, it brought into public view the threat that department cutbacks posed to the public. Perhaps for this reason, among others, the mayor's first budget restored full complements of fire fighters to twenty fire companies and reopened two firehouses, although the continued need for city fiscal restraint meant that other departments, such as police and education, had to absorb budget cuts.

There was some satisfaction in the ending of the story. Before the fire commissioner left office, his honest deputy promised us that the fire department would change the final figure for 1976 to 289. (Our 8 additional deaths would have brought the total to 290, but 1 of the deaths on the department's original list turned out to have been a duplicate.) On January 6 the *Post* reported the change and noted that the earlier 1976 mark "had been challenged by critics. Assembly-man Charles Schumer today said that the Fire Department told him it settled on the new figure." The *Daily News*, true to form on this issue, a week later announced the 1977 figure of 290 and called it "a rise of one over 1976." It never mentioned the controversy.

11

Asphalt

CORRUPTION IN THE road repair business is generally thought to be traditional. A fictional character in Mario Puzo's *The Godfather* was said to have had:

> a fleet of freight-hauling trucks that made him a fortune primarily because his trucks could travel with a heavy overload and not be stopped and fined by highway weight inspectors. These trucks helped ruin the highways and then his road-building firm, with lucrative state contracts, repaired the damage wrought. It was the kind of operation that would warm any man's heart, business of itself creating more business.

Like many other realms in which corruption is generally thought to exist, it is hard to do anything without documentary evidence of wrongdoing. It was not inevitable, then, that the New York State Assembly Subcommittee on City Management would eventually attack the prices and practices in New York City's purchasing of asphalt. But it did.

Confidential sources inside government agencies come in many varieties, from borderline neurotics to skilled analysts impelled by conscience to come forward. For some reason, perhaps for mutual support in playing somewhat dangerous roles, sources often have friends who become sources.

Our source on the asphalt purchase scandal was a friend of another of our sources. The earlier source was a skilled analyst who had helped us complete exposés of the Health and Hospitals Corporation. In the course of that investigation we demonstrated that we were conscientious about protecting him against discovery by his agency. We used code names when calling him, and we carefully reviewed any documents before releasing them to make sure there were no telltale marks that would reveal who had leaked them to us; in short, we took every possible precaution. Therefore, he felt that he could in good conscience advise his friend to come to us as well.

The friend had access to a copy of a report on asphalt purchasing written by the city's investigations department in 1975, which showed that New York City was paying much more than the going market price for asphalt. Since the city's asphalt contracts were awarded on the basis of competitive bidding, which in theory results in goods being purchased at the lowest possible price, the report suggested that price-fixing and perhaps other unsavory methods had been used to subvert the competitive bidding process. But the report, by the time the subcommittee saw it, was two years old and had never been released.

In 1975 the role of the city's investigations department remained much the same as it was when Wallace S. Sayre and Herbert Kaufman described it in 1965, in the second edition of their classic *Governing New York City* (p. 363). To have released the asphalt report on his own might have been dangerous for the investigations commissioner, although we do not know specifically why or even if that was the case. Sayre and Kaufman describe the problem as follows:

> To choose the role of the autonomous public conscience is to invite the sanctions of the Mayor (who may remove him at pleasure) and the hostility of all those powerfully placed who are, or may be, hurt by his inquiries. . . . In a climate of uncertainty, blurred choices are the mark of prudence. In the main, of course, the Commissioner must do what the Mayor permits. . . .

And as we will see, several of the asphalt suppliers to New

York City were regular political contributors, among other campaigns, to the mayoral race of 1973.

The investigations department report stressed the price differences between New York City's suppliers located in New York and New Jersey suppliers, who were charging as much as 40 percent less. It also mentioned, however, the difference in price paid to the same New York-based suppliers by New York City, on the one hand, and by corporations such as the Con Edison electric company and the Port Authority, on the other. (The Port Authority is the public agency New York and New Jersey created to oversee and maintain the port facilities and transportation terminals on either side of the Hudson River.) But the report was somewhat out of date. We had to update the figures to determine whether the apparent price-fixing still existed and then decide how to make our presentation.

The report noted that Con Edison paid about $13 a ton for asphalt in 1975, while the city was paying about $19 a ton, for effectively the same kind of asphalt and in both cases from New York suppliers. This was an outrageous differential. But when we called Con Edison to get current figures, it at first refused to supply any information on its asphalt purchase costs. Calls to higher-ups finally produced rough figures for 1976 and 1977, much closer to the city's costs in those years, but Con Edison was never able to locate for us its figures for 1975. It claimed it had lost them. This unlikely-sounding answer was the only one we ever received for this minor mystery. But our source for the investigations department report, who was to prove accurate on every subsequent matter, told us that top Con Edison officials in 1975 were the sources for the 1975 Con Edison figures. So we regarded the report's figures for Con Ed in that year as solid, although Con Edison itself would never confirm or deny them to us. As we later learned, Con Edison had had its own problems with asphalt suppliers.

The Port Authority was also reluctant to supply figures, but it did, confirming the 1975 figures in the report and adding figures for 1976 and 1977. On the average, New York City had paid $19 a ton, compared with Con Ed's $15 a ton and the Port Authority's $15.50 a ton. At the same time, the city had bought more than 1 million tons of asphalt at these prices; Con Ed and the Port Authority had purchased no more than 5,000 or 10,000 tons. Despite what therefore should have been enormous economies of scale, New York City had been paying as much as 45 percent more for its asphalt.

We decided to stress this aspect of the investigation, rather than the comparison with New Jersey prices, because we did not want to give the city or the suppliers the opportunity to confuse the issue by arguing the benefits of using New York rather than New Jersey suppliers—keeping business in New York, payroll taxes, and so forth. We had enough information to make a devastating case with what we had.

Our figures showed that if the city had bought its asphalt at the prices Con Edison or the Port Authority had paid, it would have paid about $5 million less over the course of the three years in question. The details were telling: In 1976 the city paid one supplier $18.55 a ton while the same supplier sold better asphalt to the Port Authority for less than $15 a ton.

A competitive bidding process that could produce this result had to have had something wrong with it. The history of the bidding was instructive: In 1975 the Port Authority had paid $14.15 a ton to one supplier, Mascali, but according to city records, Mascali bid $19.15 a ton—$5 more—for the city's contract, losing out to bidders averaging $18 a ton. Were Mascali and the city's other main suppliers fronts for one another or a cartel? Had Mascali never intended to obtain the city's 1975 contract—but bid high merely to make his supposed competitors' excessive bids look more legitimate and to create the illusion of real competition?

Several things pointed to this possibility. In 1975, 1976, and 1977, bids submitted to the city by these major suppliers were almost always within 10 percent, and often within 1 percent, of one another. We discovered this by going through the city's bidding records, a matter of public record. Furthermore, if the company that won the city's contract could not meet the city's demands in the course of the year, it had to designate a backup company to step in and supply the additional asphalt needed. Of the major suppliers, Jet Asphalt had been chosen by the other three big suppliers—Mascali, Willets Point, and

Asphalt Road Products—to be their backup company. Mascali, in turn, was Jet's backup plant.

Willets Point and Mascali had a business relationship that went beyond the backup situation. The Queens telephone directory in 1978 had a listing for a "Willets Point and F. Mascali," although the number had since been changed and unlisted. In 1975 Willets Point and Mascali bid together and won the city contract for night delivery of asphalt in a joint venture. Jet, Willets Point, and Mascali all had addresses within 4,000 feet of each other in Queens.

For companies that were supposed to be engaged in competition against one another for the city's contracts, they certainly gave the impression of being on friendly terms.

The winter of 1977–78 was very cold and snowy. Such conditions are bad for the roads. Cold contracts the pavement, and it cracks. Snow melts into the cracks, then freezes again, widening them. Potholes result. As a result, there is higher demand for asphalt for repairs.

By February 1978 we were ready to go with the asphalt story, and our timing was good. The week of February 6 we called Steve Wilson, the CBS-TV investigative reporter who had covered a number of our other stories, and told him our plans to go on asphalt the following week. Wilson brought his camera crew to a closed-down plant in Manhattan where the city used to make its own asphalt and taped the chairman of our subcommittee making his charges.

On Friday, February 10, we explained the story to a friendly reporter on *The New York Times*, John Kifner, on condition that he not use it until Tuesday's newspaper on February 14. We told him that we would release the story on February 13 for use on the fourteenth, but we were giving him the advantage of some extra lead time to do as much in-depth research as he wanted.

We also called Peter Smith on Friday. Smith was the mayor's new commissioner of the General Services Administration, with jurisdiction over the department responsible for buying asphalt. As we had no reason to doubt Smith's integrity or intentions, we gave him enough notice so that he could make a knowledgeable response to the press.

Smith told us he was already aware of the problem. This

may have been because he also had had access to the investigations department report. However, it is more likely that word of our snooping around the bidding files had gotten back to him, perhaps by way of a bureaucrat who understood the sensitivity of the matter. The people in charge of the files had responded quite nervously, and our research assistant who dealt with them believed they were aware that the material was explosive.

But Smith was very much on the ball. Tuesday's *Times* quoted his response to the question of whether anyone was responsible for checking to see if others were buying more cheaply than the city: "I don't know. But whether or not there was, there's going to be now." The *Times* noted that Smith had already included a provision in the spring 1978 contract requiring the suppliers to swear that they were giving the city their best price, that they were not selling to anyone else more cheaply.

The *Daily News*, without much time to research the story in advance of publication, did little more than repeat our press release. The *Post*, however, with a later deadline as an afternoon paper, added the interesting point that the previous administration had closed the city's asphalt-producing plants, despite warnings that it would ultimately have to pay higher prices to private producers. We had tipped the *Post* reporter about the city's plants to make up for giving him the story late.

The next day both the *Post* and the *News* ran editorials about the scandal. Somewhat unfairly, the *Post* said in response to Commissioner Smith, "Demanding a pledge that city suppliers will not charge less to other customers will hardly solve the problem. Plainly, municipal officials must check out the cost of all contracts by comparing prices with other private and governmental buyers."

Smith was already doing that, and considerably more. His response was so enthusiastic that it tempted us to think that with this commissioner, we didn't even need to go to the press to get action. Smith was obviously as dedicated to obtaining improvements as we were.

But that was a line of reasoning we would have been foolish to follow. First, public pressure of the kind we were generating through the press was very useful to Smith since

he could use it with recalcitrant bureaucrats to defend his actions if he needed to: "Look, we are getting killed in the
press—you've got to tell Asphalt Producer A, with whom you've
been dealing as the city's representative for umpteen years,
that times are changing, and we have no choice but to put in
this new requirement." Second, we couldn't afford to get into
the habit of trusting government officials to follow through on
their own. Third, the more press we got on one issue, the
more feared (and therefore effective) we could be on other
issues. Fourth, we remained, after all, an entity with political
interests, and publicity was therefore desirable for its own sake,
as long as it reflected well on us.

But it was a pleasure to be able to work together with
Smith. A year earlier, when we had criticized the handling of
the city's real estate auctions by the previous administration
(see Chapter 17), the apparently instinctive response we received was obfuscation and denial. The response of the new
administration, through Commissioner Smith, was quick and
positive. It would not be necessary for us to find ways to hit
the administration again and again to get action; action was
forthcoming right away.

Unfortunately it would prove difficult to achieve wholesale
victory even with the administration as our ally. The asphalt
suppliers proved to be a resourceful and effective opponent.

We got no direct response at all from the suppliers. We did
get an angry response from John Cody, president of Teamsters
Local 282, who threatened to hurt our chairman—"politically,
of course," in case we interpreted the threat as a physical one.
According to journalist Jack Newfield, Local 282 is "gangster-
ridden," and Cody has a "long criminal record." This teamster
local supplied the labor to the asphalt suppliers, and Cody
claimed that our actions could result in the loss of contracts
by the New York firms to the New Jersey suppliers, thereby
putting his union members out of work. Although this was an
aspect of the situation we had tried to downplay by stressing
the price discrepancies within New York rather than between
New York and New Jersey, Cody argued it with us.

But Cody's opponents within the union also called us and
alleged that his real gripe wasn't New Jersey competition at
all, but much more direct: Since, they alleged, he was "in bed"

with the asphalt suppliers in his own private arrangements, anything that forced them to lower their prices hurt him personally. This cast a new light on matters.

The next step was Smith's. Perhaps on the principle that one good turn deserves another, he invited us to join him in his February 25 press conference announcing major changes in the bidding requirements for the summer 1978 asphalt contract. We had found, along with Smith, that the bidding requirements were such as to exclude from the process all but the apparently favored asphalt suppliers. For instance, the producer was required to have a heated asphalt silo. Heated silos, since the days of heated trucks, were no longer really necessary, but the requirement was apparently kept because all the favored producers had heated silos and some of the potential competitors did not. This eliminated outside producers from submitting unchallengeable bids.

So Smith eliminated the heated silo requirement, eliminated the six-mile delivery requirement, included the most-favored purchaser requirement making suppliers swear that no one was getting a better price than the city, and created five contract zones in the city to give new and smaller bidders better access to the contracts for any one given zone.

Along with its coverage of Smith's reforms, the *Times* mentioned the argument about losing jobs to New Jersey that Cody had raised. It was too late for that, however, because the public by now understood that the real issue was the incredibly high prices the city was paying for asphalt. The suppliers blamed New York City's higher wage rates, electricity costs, and real estate, payroll, and corporate taxes for their higher prices. But Schumer, our subcommittee chairman, again had the last word, noting "some questions that remain unanswered: why New York City asphalt dealers charge from 45% to 125% more than New Jersey dealers; why the City's asphalt plants were all closed down in 1973; and how can we recover the millions of dollars we have overpaid?"

Smith again made the next move. Despite all his reforms, when the March 14 opening date for bids came, there were only eight bidders, all the usual previous suppliers from New York City. With all our sound and fury, with all of Smith's efforts to entice new bidders into the competition, the winners were Jet and Mascali, acting as a joint venture. Smith threw out the bids and advertised a new opening date of March 30.

This was a blockbuster. It was also obviously illegal. Before the court threw out Smith's action, one New Jersey bid finally came in, but the court retained the new bid, sealed and intact, and would not let it be opened. On April 1 the court held that Smith would have to award the contract to Jet and Mascali after all, although it commended Smith's good intentions in attempting to get the city a lower price.

This was by no means a total defeat. Jet and Mascali, for reasons that are known only to them but that could not have been unrelated to the events of the past two months, bid about 15 percent lower than the successful bid the previous year. This resulted in savings to the city of $1.5 million over what the city would probably have paid without our subcommittee's revelations.

Still, we were not willing to let our investigation drop. Like Smith, we were deeply disappointed with the results of the "reformed" bidding procedures, and we wanted to know why the cheaper New Jersey companies weren't bidding. We got some unexpected help—a telephone call from Nicholas Pileggi.

A brilliant investigative reporter, Pileggi is one of the most knowledgeable people in the country on the activities of organized crime. He was interested in our asphalt story for a possible *New York* magazine article. But when we met with him in late February, although he was the reporter and we were the sources, we learned almost as much from him as he from us.

First, we learned that we were not the first to expose price-fixing in the asphalt industry in New York. As he told us, and as we later found documented elsewhere, Con Edison was the victim of a bid-rigging scheme uncovered in 1969 which included most of the leading asphalt suppliers at that time. Since many of the companies had changed names and front men over the years, it was difficult to tell exactly which of the ones on our 1975–1977 list were represented in the 1969 arrangement, but Pileggi told us that "Tully and DiNapoli," in the 1969 group, later became known as our "Willets Point" company. So at least some of the Con Ed bid riggers caught in 1969 still seemed to be rigging bids in 1977.

Also, there was no question that the asphalt industry, as represented by the Metropolitan Asphalt Paving Association, had good political connections. As we had mentioned in our initial press release, it was never entirely clear why the city had closed down its last asphalt-producing plant in 1973. Sources in the union that used to service the city's plants told us that in the early 1970's the city's transportation administrator had warned the union that the city's plants were cost-inefficient. Apparently the plants were overstaffed with useless political appointees. The union officials involved, however, allegedly told the administrator that they wouldn't balk if the city fired all the unnecessary workers. They urged, however, that at least one plant be kept open so as not to leave the city entirely vulnerable to the private asphalt-production industry. But the administrator prevailed, and the city closed its last plant in 1973.

By all accounts the transportation administrator was completely honest, if naïve. But as Pileggi told us and later wrote in his *New York* magazine article on the subject, there was evidence of a political connection with others in the then-current (1973) and previous administrations. In 1973 officials of the Jet Asphalt Company and of Mascali and Sons testified before the Senate Watergate Committee that they had donated $10,000 in cash to the mayor's presidential campaign. Furthermore, company officials had regularly attended Democratic party fund raisers since 1966.

This testimony revealed that the $10,000 had been collected for the presidential campaign in May 1972, even though the campaign had been disbanded in April. The money had been collected by a highways department superintendent. It is a matter of record that in June 1972 Jet and Mascali won $1.7 million in city asphalt contracts. It is also a matter of record that in 1973 the last asphalt plant owned by the city, the one that the highway superintendent had been in charge of, was closed. And as a result of the subcommittee's investigation, it became a matter of public record that by 1975 Jet and Mascali were charging the city 30 to 35 percent more than they were charging their other customers.

Yet some parts of the history still eluded us. We decided to keep digging into the files and into our sources' memories.

After the investigations department report was written in 1975, bidding—which was previously limited to New York City—was opened, formally at least, to New Jersey. True, a five-mile delivery requirement was imposed, but some New Jersey plants were within five miles of New York City.

Why was any change at all made in 1975? Our sources believed that the administration threatened the suppliers with the release of the report or else simply relayed to them the fear that if they continued to be so greedy, they would inevitably be found out. Although no New Jersey bidder was accepted in 1975 or thereafter, the suppliers did drop their average price to the city slightly in 1976.

There was a New Jersey supplier in 1976, however, within the mileage requirement, who bid 40 percent below the New York price and still didn't get the contract. Out-of-town bidders on any New York City contract may be rejected, even if their bids are as much as 5 percent lower than the bids of New York companies, on the ground that the city derives economic advantages from doing business locally. But not 40 percent. So the Gallo Company in New Jersey had to be rejected on other grounds, and it was. Since Gallo was involved in a financial dispute with the New Jersey Department of Transportation, New York City decided it could reject Gallo on the basis of New Jersey's dissatisfaction. In 1977, after the dispute was resolved without Gallo's having been shown to have been in the wrong, New York City again rejected Gallo's bid, this time because its backup plant didn't have the required heated silo.

But the Metropolitan Asphalt Paving Association was beginning to get worried; the New Jersey suppliers were coming too close. In March 1977 the association's lawyer called on the mayor for a meeting and got it. In attendance were the investigations commissioner, the transportation administrator, several other high-ranking city officials, and officers of the asphalt supply companies. The suppliers said, in effect, "Don't let those New Jersey companies get the contracts." The mayor said, simply, that the letter of the law of the bidding requirements would be adhered to. According to our sources at that meeting, the mayor's statement was enough. The suppliers walked away happy.

By bidding time for the 1977 summer contract, and clearly

by 1978, when Smith appealed for New Jersey bidders, most of the New Jersey companies had given up. The one Jersey supplier who entered a bid in Smith's illegal second bidding process in 1978 appeared (briefly) on the record as the backup contractor for the 1978 Jet-Mascali contract. When our subcommittee called that company to ask about the nature of the bidding, why it and other New Jersey companies had not put in bids in the first 1978 go-round, it was extremely closed-mouthed.

Smith was forced to resign as general services commissioner during the summer of 1978 (see below). His successor assured us that he would continue Smith's efforts to open competition for the city's asphalt supply contracts.

On Thursday, March 22, 1979, we thought we saw the first fruits of our efforts to eliminate the bid specifications that had been used to deter noncartel firms. The new commissioner told us that for the first time an "outsider" firm had just submitted what looked like a successful low bid for a New York City asphalt supply contract. Bossert Asphalt of Newark, New Jersey, bid $700,000 for the contract, as against $745,000 by its only competitor, Metropolitan Asphalt Paving Company of Queens, a member of the Metropolitan Asphalt Paving Association.

Under the old bidding specifications, firms submitting bids had had to be within six miles of the city delivery point. Bossert was sixteen miles away, well within the twenty-five-mile limit of the new specifications.

Even with the less restrictive bidding requirements, however, outside firms remained reluctant to bid. Whether the city's prior record in excluding firms on one pretext or another was the discouraging factor, or whether there were other kinds of discouragement supplied perhaps by the Metropolitan Asphalt Paving Association, is open to speculation. But Bossert was the only outside firm to bid in 1979, and its success was crucial to encouraging potential future outside competitors.

So, on March 28, we publicly hailed Bossert's bid with a press release headlined "Asphalt Industry Stranglehold on NYC Contracts Broken as 'Outsider' Firm Wins Low Bid Contest." As we knew, however, and as the press release went on to explain, this was a bit premature.

Final approval for Bossert depended on a determination by the city's Board of Estimate, composed of the mayor, city council president, comptroller, and five borough presidents, under the 5 percent rule. This rule provided that if two companies bid for a city contract, and the lower bid was by a company outside the city against a city-based competitor, the lower bidder did not automatically win the contract unless his bid was more than 5 percent below the competition. If it was within 5 percent, the Board of Estimate made the decision. The rule was designed to promote industry in New York City and to counterbalance any additional costs of doing business here against the economic benefits to New York City, such as salaries for more of its residents.

Upon receiving Bossert's bid, the deputy commissioner called Bossert about what seemed to be a discrepancy in its price for one of the types of asphalt being sold. Bossert reduced its bid by another $36,000, which brought the total difference between its bid and its competitor's to more than 5 percent. In the hearing regarding the contract award, scheduled by the Board of Estimate based on the initial, less than 5 percent difference in the bids, the attorney for the Metropolitan Asphalt Paving Association argued strenuously that the deputy commissioner's action constituted a tampering with the sealed bid process. Other asphalt association representatives argued that awarding the contract to Bossert would cost the city jobs, business, and taxes and would threaten the well-being of the New York asphalt industry. (The Bossert contract was for less than 8 percent of the city's planned asphalt purchases for summer 1979—cartel members were the only bidders for all the rest.)

I testified before the board as well. I argued that the Metropolitan Asphalt Paving Association attorney's argument was a red herring; even if the bids were within 5 percent of each other, the board could and should award the contract to Bossert. I concluded, "To approve this bid means more than simply saving $100,000 for the taxpayers of this great city. It is a signal to both the New York and New Jersey asphalt contractors that we have returned to the field of open competition."

The representative of the borough president of Queens,

home of the cartel, said he couldn't understand my argument. The representative of the borough president of Brooklyn, who was apparently providing some Board of Estimate variation of legislative courtesy to his colleague from Queens, asked me if I really intended to go against the wishes of "my" borough president. He seemed to think that since the subcommittee chairman was from Brooklyn, we owed some sort of deference to the borough president of Brooklyn.

Even the representative of the city comptroller made nasty comments. This surprised some observers from the press, who told me privately that they had expected this office to be more cautious. The office had recently been badly tarred in a bus shelter scandal that linked the award of another city contract to campaign contributions to the comptroller.

The mayor's representative was conciliatory but apparently felt that he needed time to get a legal opinion on whether the deputy commissioner's actions had indeed been permissible. There was really no reason why the contract couldn't have been awarded then and there, but the board did not—or would not—understand that. The matter was deferred for two weeks.

I left the board hearing depressed and nervous, nervous that the contract would somehow slip away from Bossert before the two weeks were over. But I would be far more nervous before the day, April 5, was ended.

April 5 was a Thursday, and that year on Thursday nights at 8:00 P.M. I taught administrative law at the John Jay College of Criminal Justice. Regularly at 7:30 I would go into a bar around the corner to have a beer and review my notes. At 7:28 P.M. that day, as I was about to cross the street to the bar, a Metropolitan Asphalt Paving Company truck pulled into a no-parking space right in front of the bar.

This made me very, very nervous. I was the only one who had testified really forcefully in favor of Bossert and against awarding the contract to Metropolitan Asphalt Paving, its competitor. I stood still, on *my* side of the street.

To my utter astonishment, and considerable relief, two gentlemen emerged from the truck and began fixing the street. This is an unusual sight in the evening, but it was a very welcome one.

My own personal worries that evening turned out to have been fleeting and groundless. The matter of the contract award had a less happy resolution.

In the days immediately following April 5, we spent a great deal of time conferring with the commissioner's office at the General Services Administration and representatives of the other Board of Estimate members. It seemed that the mayor, the council president, the comptroller (after all), and at least one borough president would vote for the Bossert contract award. This would have been more than enough to assure the matter.

But on April 18, the day before the board was to make its decision, the commissioner's office gave us some very bad news. Bossert and the city had received letters from Bossert's backup supplier, the Little Ferry Asphalt Corporation, stating that it was withdrawing. The backup had backed out. Without a back-up plant, a company's bid is invalid, so Bossert was disqualified.

In the ordinary course of business there is little to be lost and much to be gained from backup status. The requirement of backup status was in many ways a vestigial one which also should have been eliminated. The cartel firms listed one another as backups, but it was very rare that the principal supplier was unable to meet its commitment to the city on a given day. On the other hand, backup status meant a firm established contact and learned the procedures of asphalt supply for the city, thereby putting it in a good position to bid for lucrative contracts the following year.

What made Little Ferry's untimely withdrawal even more suspicious was that according to the commissioner's office, the respective principals of Little Ferry and Bossert had been close personal friends for fifteen years.

Little Ferry said in its withdrawal note that it feared it could not meet the responsibilities involved in backup status. While no one was ever able to get a more specific answer from the company, we speculated that it meant that it was difficult to make asphalt with sixty bullet holes in your chest.

On May 1 we asked the investigations commissioner to examine the incident. We noted our curiosity about the fact that interest in the contracts generally was so minimal among New

Jersey suppliers and that strenuous efforts by the city to replace Little Ferry were met with nervous refusals by other New Jersey suppliers.

The investigations commissioner got nowhere, just as we had got nowhere in 1978, when we tried to question suppliers about why they hadn't bid despite Smith's efforts to create more open competition. All of the thirty or so New Jersey suppliers the subcommittee tried to question were disinclined to talk. In other investigations, when a subcommittee exposé received the kind of massive press coverage that the asphalt scandal did, new informants would come out of the woodwork, offering us additional information on the subject at hand. In fact, we had sort of counted on such informants to fill some of the gaps in our knowledge of the asphalt story. But this time our efforts were greeted with silence.

At the risk of sounding melodramatic, it is not hard to theorize that *omertà*, the Mafia pledge of silence, would describe the situation. No evidence of Mafia connections ever came into our possession. However, the teamster official who had threatened the subcommittee chairman over the telephone was subsequently the subject of a thorough analysis by Jack Newfield in the *Village Voice* (December 6, 1978, "This Felon Controls the Most Corrupt Union in New York").

Furthermore, Newfield's piece corroborated the dissident teamsters' allegations that the union leadership was in bed with the asphalt suppliers: The union shop steward and the owner of Willets Point, through their wives, are partners in a trucking company. Since Cody's control of the union is total, this may help explain his outrage over our attack on the owners' interests.

Newfield also wrote that Cody had been arrested for violent crimes on numerous occasions; Cody's chauffeur, who doubled as a business agent for the union, was charged with murder but was himself murdered, his body found, on June 6, 1974, stuffed in a car trunk before he could be tried; an official greeter at the wedding of Cody's son was Carlo Gambino, the late Mafia Godfather; and another business agent for the local was Harry Gross, a former associate in Murder, Inc.

The unofficial and undocumented but universal opinion of our sources also was that this was indeed an industry with strong connections with organized crime. And the very peculiar silence from the industry that followed our revelations could only add to our suspicions along those lines.

We never got to the bottom of the asphalt story. The few thousand dollars in campaign contributions that the industry gave to the 1973 mayoral race really did not seem adequate to explain the failure of the administration to take action, the investigations commissioner's decision not to release the investigations department report, and the failure of every other possible watchdog agency in the city, including the comptroller's office, to spot this obvious rip-off of the city's treasury.

We did, however, cost the asphalt industry about $1.5 million in excess profits it would probably otherwise have been able to extract from the city in 1978. And then, on December 20, 1979, we won the victory we had announced prematurely: Little Ferry bid for and won the 1980 winter contract for Manhattan against the Metropolitan Asphalt Paving Association contender. Whether the inquiry into its withdrawal as backup the previous year somehow heartened it enough to try a bid on its own we'll probably never know, but the ice was broken— and with it the previously invulnerable grip of the Metropolitan Asphalt Paving Association cartel on the city's contracts.

And our intervention had one more result—the most important of all. As we continued to probe the files of the departments of purchase and transportation during the summer of 1978, we heard from employees that the city was planning to make its own asphalt again. This, the most radical of our recommendations, would be most effective in freeing the city from dependence on private suppliers. Indeed, this would undo the trap that the suppliers had set for the city when they had apparently influenced policy makers to close the last city plant in 1973.

In September the mayor promised that the city would build its own plants to compete with the cartel. By May 1979, after the Bossert incident, we knew that this was our last best hope of escape from the cartel's grip. Yet seeing how the Bossert contract had slipped away, we vowed to exercise full vigilance over the playing out of this matter.

The mayor's budget for fiscal year 1980 did not pass easily. The mayor had included an appropriation for an asphalt plant.

However, we were warned that such an item had been in the budget in the previous two years but had not survived the attentions of the Queens borough president during the budget negotiation process.

Throughout June 1979 we called the office of the highways commissioner to monitor the progress of the plant. The office assured us that this time the plant would go through. We assured the staff that if it didn't, we would see to it that there was hell to pay.

It went through.

People who assumed that the asphalt industry did, in fact, have a connection with organized crime, have often asked me whether I or the subcommittee chairman ever felt we were in personal physical danger.

The answer, even assuming such a connection, is that there probably was no such danger. The powers involved undoubtedly continue to make enormous amounts of money on other contracts with the city. Pileggi, in the June 19 and June 26, 1978, issues of *New York* magazine, later exposed, for example, organized crime involvement in millions upon millions of dollars of school busing contracts. All this money is made without anybody's getting hurt. From the point of view of the intelligent mob chieftain—and anyone capable of winning and keeping such contracts for so many years is not likely to be stupid —it is not worth killing anyone, particularly not a government official, to protect a fraction of the profits that will continue to come in.

The Arizona experience, mentioned in Chapter 2, is instructive. There reporter Don Bolles was blown up by a bomb placed in his car in 1976 while he was investigating organized crime in that state. Public reaction to that murder—unlike public reaction to the more customary murders of mobsters by other mobsters—was so intense that investigative reporters from all over the country descended on Arizona to crack the organized crime involvement there. Financial and political operations of organized crime were exposed at the highest levels, and the financial and political careers of many ambitious mob-connected individuals were ruined.

It is unlikely that the lesson was lost on mobsters elsewhere. Nothing the Arizonians were trying to protect by killing Don Bolles could have been worth the price they had to pay for that killing. The moral for investigators is ironically reassuring: The mob will undoubtedly keep on making enough money, despite your investigations, for it to be uneconomical for them to kill you.

Of course, should you encounter a crazy or stupid mobster, there might be danger. But as I said above, it is very unlikely that any mobsters with lucrative government contracts are stupid or crazy.

It may be that the mob has other means of revenge for those with certain vulnerabilities. Our ally in the asphalt fight, Peter Smith, was forced to resign as general services commissioner in the summer of 1978, before we achieved our final victory. Serious legal questions were raised about certain financial practices in which he had engaged prior to his appointment. Although the transactions in question took place while he was in a private, nongovernmental capacity, they raised questions of such gravity that his continued retention as commissioner would have been an untenable embarrassment to the mayor.

The theory has been floated that the interests Smith so energetically and courageously attacked while commissioner may have seen to it that these questions about his past were raised. This is highly speculative since the incidents could have surfaced in any number of ways. Still, for those who do not believe in accidents, the powerful enemies Smith surely made in the asphalt industry offer a convenient explanation for his exposure.

As for us on the subcommittee, since there are no skeletons in our closets, we should have had nothing to worry about on that score. And since it would have been irrational for anyone to take physical vengeance on us, we should have had no worries on that score either. Somehow, though, the myth—if that's what it was—of Mafia involvement in the asphalt industry lent this particular investigation of ours an atmosphere of—let's say —*interest* above and beyond the usual. . . .

12

Deaths at a City Hospital

JOHN ROBERTS (not his real name) was a former social worker at one of the city hospitals. He was young, good-looking, articulate, and intelligent but had a kind of neurotic intensity that worried me. During the summer of 1977 he had sent documentation of mismanagement at his hospital to various public officials, often accompanied by the kind of poorly typewritten cover notes that legislators usually receive from cranks—inappropriate underlining, exclamation points, and capitalized words. Nonetheless, Roberts's notes were coherent. The following January Roberts was fired from the hospital, allegedly for refusing to take psychiatric tests.

At the end of 1977 our Subcommittee on City Management had released a detailed report on waste and mismanagement at the Health and Hospitals Corporation, identifying $28 million of waste in one year because of incompetence. The report received considerable news and editorial coverage, prompting a number of people, including Roberts, to contact us to report their own observations of the city's hospital system.

Many of these new informants called to report mistreatment in their own individual cases. Even fully documented, these were not appropriate for subcommittee investigation unless they showed an unmistakable pattern. John Roberts, however, reported mismanagement on a large scale and came complete with documentary support.

Even so, at first it was hard to avoid writing him off as a nut who had been fired and was now taking revenge. Roberts's intense and nervous presentation of his story added to our skepticism. But the documents seemed irrefutable.

The lead memorandum was from Roberts to the executive director of the hospital, noting that at least two patients had died in the confusion of moving them from wards 4 South and 3 East. The second memorandum—from Dr. Canute Bernard, physician and chairperson of the hospital's community board, to the hospital's executive director—described the circumstances preceding the deaths of four patients on 4 South, including missed dosages of medication and seriously delayed surgical procedures. The third memorandum, by the hospital's medical director, provided qualifying information, such as explaining away equipment breakdowns which could have occurred "in any institution." But it effectively corroborated the second memorandum.

The subcommittee had a special reason for making a *cause célèbre* out of this. The executive director of the hospital at that time had since been promoted to the first vice-presidency of the entire Health and Hospitals Corporation, the central hierarchy of which we had found to be uncommonly inept. But it was so well protected politically that even the newly elected mayor was unable to take decisive action to remove it. We hoped that this exposé, by revealing the director's poor past performance (which had not prevented a major promotion), would weaken the central hierarchy.

Roberts also told us that while the hospital had been suffering from staffing shortages which contributed to patient deaths, the director had authorized the construction of a $3,000 door to his office, among other lavish and luxurious items. We hoped to use that incident to underscore the inadequacy of "tight budgets" as an excuse for the city hospitals.

Before moving on the story, however, our chairman (Charles Schumer) insisted we get some corroboration to cover the outside possibility that Roberts had forged the memorandums. So we called the author of the third memorandum, the hospital's former medical director, who Roberts had indicated was nervous but honest. He certainly was both, telling us that he had indeed written the memorandum but refusing to discuss it.

The subcommittee staffer who had been assigned to the

project also called the assistant director of the hospital, who confirmed that nursing shortages remained a critical problem that had never been remedied. Another source of information became available to us when we realized that the sister of a friend of the subcommittee staff worked in one of the laboratories at the hospital. She put us in touch with yet another hospital employee whose sick infant had been misdiagnosed because of the staffing shortage.

Roberts had gone to a great many legislators with his memoranda but had obviously been written off as a crank. Until he came to us, no one had taken effective action on the basis of his complaints. He came to us in early January, and when we had still not moved four weeks later, he began to lose confidence in us as well.

In mid-February three deaths at a hospital in Queens became the subject of a homicide investigation by the Queens district attorney. The press coverage was tremendous. This was our cue that the timing was right for our charges. On February 21, we accompanied Roberts's memoranda with a press release that read: "Allegations of Negligence in Patient Deaths Spread to Second Queens Hospital: Confidential Hospital Memoranda Attribute 5 Deaths to Mismanagement, Overcrowding, Nursing Shortages."

It was the credo of the subcommittee that no charges were made unless we had complete and irrefutable documentation for every allegation. Otherwise, credibility could have been lost. So when I got a call from a friend on the New York *Post*, several hours after the release went out, saying that he could find references to only *four* patient deaths, not five, in Roberts's memoranda, the shock was devastating. To an outsider, the difference between four and five deaths in the circumstances described seems small, but to a professional reformer, it is everything. If the subcommittee could be wrong about the number of deaths, couldn't it be wrong about the more complex matter of analyzing the causes of those deaths? And would not its judgment in holding the city hospitals accountable also be much less worthy of respect?

The subcommittee staffer who had prepared the analysis and first draft of the press release was unusually careful and thorough. Nevertheless, I had established a rule that no factual allegation be made unless I personally checked the substantiation for it. Indeed, on an earlier draft I had corrected the staffer's death count from six to five, but I should have changed it to four. (Since Roberts's memoranda referred to the patients in different ways, it was not immediately obvious how many deaths there had been.)

After the *Post* reporter's call and a rereading of Roberts's memoranda, we had to agree that there were only four.

That wasn't our only problem, though. Our chairman's hunch on checking the memorandums for authenticity now seemed to have been intuitive. Dr. Canute Bernard, the author of the second memorandum, was telling the press that he could not recall having written or signed the memorandum—although it had been signed—and he therefore could not comment on its truth.

Only two things kept us from hysteria. First, we had obtained corroboration of the third memorandum. Secondly, our friend on the *Post* said he would ignore the discrepancy, write his story using *four* deaths, and recommend to the editors that they not give it too much prominence since he was not sure of its accuracy.

By 10:00 P.M. the Night Owl edition of the *Daily News* was out. Across the front page was the banner headline "5 Deaths Blamed on Hospital." On page 3 was a long story with a picture: excellent coverage under ordinary conditions. This time it raised our level of nervousness to unbearable heights. What if our mistake became public knowledge?

The following day, although we had not thought it possible, the level of tension was raised again. Wednesday's *Daily News* story was headlined "[Mayor] Asks Report in 5 Hospital Deaths." Again, under ordinary circumstances, this would have been the best possible response we could have gotten: the newly elected mayor immediately demanding an explanation from the city hospitals for the serious issues we had raised. But in this case we were afraid. The results of the investigation could show the mayor that we were careless and wrong.

The *News* editorial that day also gave us support that we were not sure we deserved. It said:

In short, the whole grim business seems to point to one

main cause—mismanagement from the top down. The top, in this case, is the city's Health and Hospitals Corporation. Its first move after Schumer's charge was to deny all, and to suggest that the documents may have been forged.

We were seriously worried that Bernard's memorandum might indeed have been written by someone else—specifically, Roberts. Bernard's explanation to us that memoranda from him as chairman of the hospital's community board were frequently written by someone else for his signature had the ring of truth. We suspected that Roberts, who had been chairman of a patient care committee, could have written this one.

We felt very much under the gun, under time pressure to substantiate our story. We had to present our strongest case to the mayor before the Health and Hospitals Corporation took advantage of our errors to hurt our credibility.

We didn't want to seek any more information from Roberts at this point because we felt he might alter information to substantiate his charges. Our source in the laboratory proved a real godsend—she found us an employee with access to the hospital's "death book."

Hospitals generally keep a list of patient deaths in chronological order. This information, like all patient information, is confidential. But we had to make sure that at least four patients had really died the way the memorandums said they did. We were also afraid that the hospital might even destroy or alter its records so that no proof of the deaths we alleged would be found.

The employee with the death book first told us that she could find no deaths under the chart numbers on the memoranda. After we pleaded for further efforts—she was engaging in a highly dangerous activity on our behalf—she finally found one patient death description that matched one of ours: during the moves in wards 4 South and 3 East. But she was afraid to spend any more time looking at the death book for fear she might be seen. Instead, she went one step better—she smuggled the book out of the hospital for us to examine ourselves.

We found all *five* deaths. True, there were only four clear death descriptions in the three memorandums Roberts had given us. But the memorandum Roberts had written had referred to deaths resulting from the confusion in moving patients in wards 4 South *and 3 East*; the four deaths Dr. Bernard described subsequently were only Ward 4 South patients. The death book listed another in the right time period in 3 East. It is embarrassing to admit that the discovery of someone's death can result in great exhilaration, but honest reporting of this investigation demands that admission.

As our fear subsided and logic returned, we realized that Roberts could not have written the Bernard memorandum. Roberts was intelligent but could not have used the medical terminology in the memorandum. Whether Bernard wrote it or not, a doctor did; for our peace of mind, that was all we needed to know. But we learned more.

We spoke with several persons who had been members of the community board at the time. While they didn't know whether Bernard had written the memorandum himself, they did know that he had argued against its release at a community board meeting and had been outvoted. To imply, as he had, that he knew nothing of its contents was misleading at best.

So we were back on solid ground. One more piece of good luck—or rather one more good source—brought us the report that Joseph Lynaugh, the acting president of the Health and Hospitals Corporation, had sent to the mayor to refute our allegations.

Sources were the key to this investigation. Roberts, of course, initiated the matter. The woman with the misdiagnosed infant confirmed the persistence of the problems. The employee with the death book saved our credibility. Members of the community board cleared up our worries about Bernard and supplied us with additional and more current records. Once an investigation of a scandalously run institution begins, conscientious people throughout the institution help bring out the truth. It is a profoundly heartening phenomenon.

As we had expected, Lynaugh's first response was to attack our credibility by challenging us on the number of deaths. His first point was to allege that the third memorandum, by the medical director, did not find "any relationship between these deaths and deficiencies in the care provided," and "only four deaths were described . . . rather than five patients as alleged by Assemblyman Schumer." His second point was that whatever problems did exist at the time of the deaths had been addressed and corrected by management.

Our later research into the number of deaths recorded in the death book enabled us to turn the credibility issue around entirely. The Roberts reference to the situation in Ward 3 East enabled us to reply to the mayor:

> A close reading of the memoranda will show references to 5 deaths, as indicated by Assemblyman Schumer's February 21 press release. . . . An additional hospital memorandum which we had also located subsequently documents the death of patient J.G. . . . on ward 3E during the period of time under discussion. . .

Lynaugh's response to the third memorandum was very misleading. Indeed, that memorandum had not explicitly stated that there was a relationship between the deaths and the deficiencies in care we noted. But it did state:

> There is little doubt that the nursing shortage has been so severe as to result in missed doses. . . .
> There is little doubt that patient care has been significantly diminished by the sharp reduction in nurses, aides, orderlies, and technicians.

And with respect to one patient:

> [T]his patient did not receive adequate nursing attention in that orders were not picked up and she did not receive the required nursing care on the ward. This is probably absolutely true [sic]. . . . Anyone studying the nurse-to-patient ratio in this hospital and taking into account the nature of the patients will immediately realize that we are below any acceptable nationwide standard.

We pointed out to the mayor that it was not logical of Lynaugh to assert that these conditions did not contribute to patient deaths. We also pointed to a letter written by the vice-president of an affiliated hospital, seven months *after* the deaths, charging that the hospital's director "in the face of the need to cut patient service programs . . . continues to add administrators to his staff." Finally, we cited a city health department inspection a year later noting continued inadequacies in nursing and medical staff coverage.

We sent our reply to the mayor on March 3, 1978. There was no immediate response. But on May 19 *Newsday* reported that the city's Health and Hospitals Corporation, "declaring a state of emergency at Queens Hospital Center, replaced the hospital's acting head with a permanent executive director yesterday and appropriated $1 million to help improve services there. . . ."

Patient deaths attributable to mismanagement are not an unusual story in any hospital, and it is probable that they are a very common story at municipal hospitals. Emergency help for and reorganization of one municipal hospital in Queens were hardly a major reform of the city's hospitals, but they were the goal of our exposé, and they were achieved.

This provided an ironic contrast with the results of our much more extensive exposé of the overall Health and Hospitals Corporation budget, mentioned earlier. This December 1977 report had said mismanagement was costing the city at least $28 million in one year. When the mayor-to-be, then two weeks short of his swearing-in, was asked about the subcommittee's findings, he said that he was not surprised and that he planned to ask the state legislature to restructure or abolish the Health and Hospitals Corporation, as reported in *The New York Times* on December 20, 1977.

But after the mayor's inauguration, things didn't go quite that way. The media reported that the mayor was planning to oust Lynaugh and make Axel Schupf president of the Health and Hospitals Corporation. This also failed to occur. Instead, Lynaugh remained as president and Schupf became chairman of the board, until then a less powerful position than president. For several months Lynaugh continued to hold the reins of the organization.

In January I had met with Lynaugh's deputy over the allegations made by the subcommittee on the $28 million wasted. The deputy had offered to supply documentation to demonstrate that the matters the subcommittee had raised were already undergoing reform. On January 13 we sent the deputy a letter requesting that documentation. By July Lynaugh's deputy had not yet responded. Common Cause, following up in July on the subcommittee's work, found that merchandise procurement reforms that the deputy had reported verbally at our meeting had simply never taken place.

In August Axel Schupf fired Lynaugh's deputy, signaling that Lynaugh's regime was coming to an end. But Schupf resigned first because of a combination of his own blunders and effective undercutting by Lynaugh. Not until the end of 1978 did the mayor finally ask Lynaugh for his resignation. Why had it taken so long?

The Health and Hospitals Corporation has a budget of roughly $1.5 billion a year. This enables it to hire a great many people. Among them are many members of AFSCME District Council No. 37, the union of municipal employees. When the mayor first attempted to replace Lynaugh with Schupf, he was also in the process of negotiating with Washington for aid to New York City and of negotiating with the unions for their new city contracts. The union's pension funds played an important role in the financial plan the city had to show the federal government. The head of the union and a key union pension fund consultant (who spoke for all municipal unions on this subject) were staunch allies of Lynaugh's. The precise manner in which these two men saved Lynaugh from termination the first time the mayor tried to remove him is not known, but all the readings of political scuttlebutt indicate that save him they did.

It seemed ironic that the subcommittee exposé of $28 million of waste and all sorts of egregious mismanagement—in a somewhat limited analysis of only part of the Health and Hospital Corporation's operations—produced no visible result except, ironically, the departure of the corporation's public relations officer. Because of good press timing and the intrinsic human drama of the issue, the hospital deaths story—though of far less significance to the management of the city's hospital system—had a much more concrete and immediate impact. And it may well have undercut any efforts by Lynaugh to establish credibility with the mayor because we were able to make Lynaugh's response look self-serving and foolish.

Gradually even Lynaugh's political allies seemed to realize that he was not the right person for the job. By October our private discussions with union leaders indicated a decline in Lynaugh's standing with them because of his perceived incompetence. By early 1979 he was gone.

Obviously that did not mean that Armageddon was at hand and the city hospitals were cleaned up. Indeed, the next act would produce hospital budget cuts and closings throughout the city. But we did encourage the city to produce some improvement at the Queens Hospital Center, and we surely contributed to the beginning of the end of the Lynaugh administration. Both seemed worthy victories.

13

Stalking Mosquitoes with a Shotgun

In the early summer of 1977 on my way to my office in the State Office Building, across the street from City Hall, I met an old college friend who suggested, "Look, if you want a real scandal to investigate, check into the fees the city pays its expert witnesses in tax certiorari cases."

Tax certiorari cases concern the city's assessments of real estate. Initially a property is assessed by an employee of the Finance Administration, and the real estate tax paid is a percentage (about 9 percent) of the "assessed value" of the property. The property owner who thinks the assessment is too high, requiring a higher tax than he or she feels is justified, may appeal to the city's Tax Commission. The Tax Commission is independent of the Finance Administration, and its members are appointed directly by the mayor and serve part time at the pleasure of the mayor.

Decisions of the Tax Commission may be appealed by the property owner to the Appellate Division of the Supreme Court of New York State. These appeals are called tax certiorari proceedings. At that stage property owners often bring in real estate appraisers who serve as expert witnesses to testify that the assessments are too high. The city does the same, except that its witnesses testify that the assessments are correct or perhaps too low.

Our source's tip concerned the fees paid to these witnesses

149

by the city. He was not very specific, but he indicated that they were paid a tremendous amount of money under somewhat questionable circumstances.

First, we located the branch of the Appellate Division in which these cases were heard. From the clerk of that court, we got the list of appraisers hired by the city as expert witnesses in the cases. The list was short. Only twelve names appeared on it regularly. The next job was to find out how much money each appraiser received.

The comptroller's office must approve the voucher for every payment the city makes. In the musty basement of an old city office building near City Hall are perhaps millions of vouchers recording the history of the city's transactions. We found the vouchers for the expert witnesses.

Of several hundred independent appraisers in the city in 1977, only about a dozen got all the work—and the bulk of that went to three men: Samuel Simms earned a total of $231,000 in expert witness fees for testifying in 127 tax certiorari cases. Stanley Siebert received $108,000, and H. R. Mandel received $33,000. These three men shared an office. Of the $514,000 that the city paid out in such fees in 1977, these men received 73 percent. What service did Samuel Simms provide that the city should have paid him more than three times the mayor's salary in that year?

While there was no indication that Simms and his associates were incompetent, there was also no indication that they were outstandingly successful in winning cases for the city. This looked to us like evidence of a scandal. What inside track did Simms and his associates have to get these contracts? To know this, we had to find out how expert witnesses were selected.

Our discoveries only added to our suspicions. We had a subcommittee staff member pretend to be a real estate appraiser looking for expert witness work from the city. He called the director at the corporation counsel's office who had been in charge of expert witness assignments since at least 1969. Our staff member was told: (1) There were no specific guidelines or procedures for selection; (2) there was "negotiation to a degree," presumably meaning some kind of bidding for the work, but this was so unclear as to be doubtful; (3)

the question was academic because the corporation counsel did not need any new appraisers; and (4) the director faced "other handicaps" in the selection process. He did not explain this comment.

This reply raised several questions. First, the selection procedure was obviously neither open nor fair and thus looked suspicious. Secondly, the size of the fees and the permanence of the small group receiving them made us wonder about the objectivity of their testimony as supposedly impartial witnesses. Wouldn't these factors also have hurt their credibility in court? Finally, it was hard to believe that the city could not purchase this service for less than the enormous amount of money it was paying to the favored witnesses.

In our handling of this exposé we decided to try an experiment. We wanted big press coverage of the story to encourage the city to reform the process. And we knew that a good technique for maximizing press coverage was the exclusive. In an exclusive, you give the story to only one reporter. Naturally, after the story appears, it is then fair game for any other reporters who wish to cover it. But the reporter—and the publication—guaranteed the exclusive are supposed to be grateful and to give the story better coverage as a result. So goes the theory, and it undoubtedly works sometimes.

Thinking we had uncovered a juicy scandal, we gave a *Times* reporter the basic outlines of the story. Since it was a fairly complicated and technical matter, we wanted her to have plenty of time to do whatever research and analysis she needed. Meanwhile, we used what we thought were the last few days before the story broke to try to find the political connections between the favored expert witnesses and the regular Democratic machine organization which was so deeply entrenched in the administration. From informal testimony we received, it seemed clear that the director who gave out the appraisal contracts was well connected in the Queens Democratic organization. (He was later awarded a position with the State Liquor Authority.) But try as we might, we could find no real evidence linking Simms, Siebert, or Mandel to any political machine.

The *Times* reporter who wrote the story took a very long time, perhaps hoping that someone would finally come up with the missing political link. By the time it was ready to go to press the city had long since figured out what we were up to. The corporation counsel had his response ready. In the *Times* of July 22, 1977, placed none too prominently, was the none too thrilling headline "City Does Much Business with Just a Few Appraisers." In addition to reporting our findings, the *Times* reported that the corporation counsel had already moved to reform the process by taking it out of the former director's hands and setting up a blue-ribbon panel to examine and assign expert witnesses. Of the few men who had been getting all the work, the corporation counsel said, "They're older men, very experienced, but there's got to be a better way of doing this."

The New York *Post* also covered the story—in a way that looked as if it were taking revenge on us for giving the exclusive to the *Times*. After all, if we were doing the *Times* a favor, we were doing the *Post* an equivalent nonfavor. It would have been bad enough if the *Post* had ignored us altogether, but what it did was worse. On page 77 it ran a story headlined "City Acting to Spread Appraiser $." The only reference to the subcommittee was a note that the corporation counsel had discovered the practice, which was going to be changed, "after a Brooklyn Assemblyman began making inquiries." No name. The assemblyman referred to was naturally our chairman. This, to a politician, is the unkindest cut of all. Later our friends at the *Post* assured us that no malice had been intended, but this was hard for us to believe.

Despite intensive research, we found no evidence that improprieties underlay the selection of the appraisers under the old system. Rather, it appeared that indeed, the city had a small pool from which to choose. An anonymous industry spokesperson was quoted in the *Times* article as saying that "most guys would rather not do court work, and they could make more on the other side of the table in these cases." Simms, with his lion's share of the business, was atypical. Per case, the private side was much more lucrative.

Under these circumstances, it may even have been economical for the city to give so much of its work to only three appraisers. The three did so much work and had done it for so long that they could probably do the average case faster and cheaper than others could.

Our intended reform of the selection process would probably not be much of an improvement. By treating the situation as a scandal rather than as a systematic problem within the economic structure of the appraisal industry, we were using tools that could not do the job.

Within a few days of the appearance of our story in the *Times* and *Post*, we found a practical solution. The root of the problem was that the city had to hire expert witnesses for a court proceeding. Resolving the facts without those witnesses would mean tremendous savings. The solution was to remove the determination of the correct assessment to an administrative forum.

A standard doctrine of American law holds that if an administrative body is created to resolve and decide certain technical issues—in this case, the assessment of a piece of property —the courts should not replace the expert judgment of the administrative body with their own judgment. If a court finds that an administrative body acted unfairly, the court remands the case back to that body for a new decision.

Thus, we proposed that a Property Tax Review Board be established as a division of the Tax Commission to hear appeals from the commission's initial rulings. The board would consist of two professional appraisers with at least ten years of experience and an attorney with at least ten years of experience in real estate law. All three would receive annual salaries of $45,000. The selection process, including public announcements and the participation of professional appraisal organizations, would be designed to ensure that the board members would be of the highest caliber and integrity and as independent of political influence as is possible for mayoral appointees.

Property owners could bring their expert witnesses and attorneys before the board. The city, however, would continue to be represented by the corporation counsel and would call on its Finance Administration employees who had done the initial assessment to testify on its behalf. The city could rely on the professional ability of the board to make fair and accurate appraisals on the basis of testimony and reports of the city assessors as well as findings of fact by the board's own staff.

Property owners would retain the right to appeal the findings of the board to court, but the court would only review the record. Should the court find that no substantial evidence supported the decision of the board, or that the board had wrongfully excluded evidence that should have been heard, the court would simply remand the case back to the board for rehearing.

The city's use of expert witnesses cost about twice as much as the board would each year, including staff. On this basis alone, not counting the opportunity cost realized by reducing some of the court caseload, the city would save $250,000 a year.

Our press release on the board proposal got no coverage. It was the first time we held a press conference and no one came. Our one bite at the apple had been our original story. Had we treated it as a management problem to which we had had a solution, the problem and the solution might have been covered in one story. As it was, lacking coverage for the solution, we failed to generate public pressure in its favor.

Interesting subsequent developments shed light on the handling of this kind of problem by public servants of integrity. The panel that the corporation counsel had assigned to examine and assign expert witnesses included at least two longtime and able civil servants, the finance administrator and an executive assistant at the office of the corporation counsel. They and several others met with Schumer and me in the fall of 1977, some months after our exposé, because they wanted to consider our board proposal, even though we had failed to generate public pressure for it.

Since our proposal met with their approval, we agreed to get more information on its implementation. We found that a similar system had been used successfully in California for at least twenty years, and we forwarded information on the California system to the Finance Administration. In December the Finance Administration advised us that pushing through a major administrative change would be more successful after the settling in of the new mayoral administration in January.

However, the new mayor gave his own Office of Management and Budget the responsibility for determining reforms in the tax certiorari system. For the next six months we attempted to communicate our proposal to the Office of Management and Budget, with no visible signs of progress.

In July 1978 State Comptroller Arthur Levitt released an audit criticizing the expert witness selection process between 1975 and 1977. The *Times* covered the story on July 4, and on July 5 the *Post* editorial page noted that Levitt had blown the whistle on this practice. I called the corporation counsel to find out if anything was being done with our board proposal in light of the new interest in the subject. The executive assistant who had previously been interested must have had too many things on her mind. She explained that if I would send her a memorandum outlining the legal steps necessary to implement the reforms I sought, she might be able to look it over in a month or so.

On July 17 the *Post* put the following letter from Schumer in a prominent box on its letters page:

> In your editorial entitled "Mr. Levitt's appraisal" (July 5) you noted that the State Comptroller "blew the whistle" on the City Law Dept.'s practice of distributing appraisal work to a small pre-selected list of appraisers.
>
> Actually, after my subcommittee blew the same whistle a year ago, then-Corporation Counsel W. Bernard Richland, much to his credit, quickly ended the practice. However, the city has thus far failed to implement (or reject) the proposal I made at that time to establish an administrative board that would replace altogether the hiring of individual appraisers. . . . It would be unfortunate if our proposal died of bureaucratic inertia when it could provide the city with significant savings.

The very next day the director of the Office of Management and Budget had hand delivered a letter in which he assured us that our proposal was still under consideration. He hoped to have necessary legislation prepared for the 1979 legislative session.

Within a few more days the executive assistant at the office of the corporation counsel called me back to ask for a note from the subcommittee on our plan, which she said was of great interest to the new corporation counsel and the new head of the Tax Commission. On August 2 I sent her a brief note on the legislative amendment needed to provide the legal basis for the board proposal. She promised a meeting with the corporation counsel within two months to work out the mechanics of implementation. Meanwhile, she explained, a tripartite board within the Tax Commission had been activated. This was expected to do many of the things we had recommended and should result in the final resolution of most of the cases that had previously gone to the Appellate Division.

As it happened, a great deal more work had to be done, and it became obvious that we were going to have to do it. So we did. With the help of our bill-drafting office, we finally came up with a legislative proposal that included the twenty pages of legal detail that would make implementation possible. In November 1979 the highly regarded new president of the Tax Commission commended our proposal to the City Club, an important civic group interested in the issue, and it appeared that the city would help push our bill through the legislature.

So we ended up with good prospects of winning the tax certiorari reform battle. The few expert witnesses now in use by the city are picked in a fair and open manner, and soon perhaps the city will eliminate the need for them altogether.

But what did this victory represent? We never found evidence of corruption or bribery in the award of expert witness fees. We found a problem in the structure of the system: a rarely looked-at corner of the government in which things had been done in an inefficient way for a long time because none of the people on the inside had much incentive to change it.

It was clearly useful for an investigative subcommittee to have had an incentive to look for problems like this one to solve; our political incentive was publicity, which went hand in hand with our idealistic motivations toward improving government operations. It taught us, though, that not every problem that looks like a scandal *is* one: sometimes unexamined inefficiencies persist by inertia. The best way to handle them is to analyze them well enough to offer a solution, then to offer the solution at the same time you expose the problem, generating maximum publicity and pressure for change. Although it appears that our plan will be adopted after all, we should have arranged better odds.

This was a small victory. But along with our auction reforms (see Chapter 17), it helped us feel that we were getting on the scoreboard, winning a few points for the public in the arena of the city government real estate operations.

14

Computers and Welfare

ONE OF THE RESPONSIBILITIES of New York City's welfare department was to handle the processing of food stamps. Because these stamps were a valuable commodity on the black market, losses through theft and fraud were frequent. Eventually someone in the welfare department thought it might be a good idea to keep a watch on the food stamp validation forms to prevent their being stolen when regular personnel were off duty.

The validation forms were kept on a desk in an office that was locked when unattended. In a flashy gesture, welfare installed a camera—of the type used for surveillance in banks—to focus on the desk and record anyone approaching the validation forms after office hours.

Predictably, for a long time no personnel were assigned to man the camera, so no films were made. One weekend, however, when the office was supposed to be empty and locked, the department finally ran the camera and processed the film.

What did the film show? A hand moving the camera to shift its focus from the validation forms on the desk to an innocuous file cabinet. For the remaining length of the film, only the file cabinet was recorded.

To me this story typified the frustration I felt whenever I thought of the welfare department. Our subcommittee's investigation of possible mismanagement in this department turned out to be one of the most baffling, complex, time-consuming, and irritating of the many cases we had covered.

What we were up against here was a monster organization.

New York City's welfare budget was over $2 billion annually. The department had dozens of offices and bureaus—including some sixty welfare centers—scattered all over the city. And it had thousands of employees engaged in serving 800,000 recipients benefiting from a variety of assistance programs. Attempting to penetrate a system of such enormous size and complexity frequently left us confused. Were we dealing with mismanagement, fraud, incompetence, ignorance? Did anyone, even in the welfare department, really know what was going on?

Another stumbling block in dealing with welfare was that client case records were confidential. This policy made it difficult to verify claims by welfare administrators of how well their departments were run. When confronted with an investigation such as ours, welfare officials, under the guise of protecting the privacy of recipients, could effectively stymie examination of records.

Finally, we were confounded by new technology—welfare was using computers. Between our own lack of expertise with computers and the department's penchant for secrecy, we bogged down in inexplicable statistics. Resolution seemed impossible without the welfare department's cooperation—hardly an ideal setup for an objective investigation.

Our involvement started one day in May 1978, when a report flew over the partition separating my desk from the rest of the office. I did not see who threw it. Therefore, I could say that I lacked certain knowledge of its source. However, that source had been standing in front of my desk thirty seconds earlier, telling me he was extremely nervous because he feared serious reprisals if he were caught.

The report concerned the welfare department's efforts to track down recipients who were illegally receiving welfare while they were also earning a living. This report, a draft titled "Social Security Number Integrity," had been prepared by the welfare department's Office of Loss Analysis and Prevention (OLAP). Basically it explained that the computerized system intended to catch welfare cheats by matching Social Security numbers of recipients with wage earners was faulty. This was startling because Social Security numbers were welfare's proclaimed "unique identifiers," and the computerized system was the department's pride. In fact, the new welfare administrator had promised the City Council that this system would save the city $10 million.

The way the system was supposed to work was that people who applied for welfare had their Social Security numbers punched into the computer. (Under federal law, welfare recipients are required to have Social Security numbers.) The numbers were then matched in New York and in Washington with those of wage earners. Thus, for example, Charlie Jones with Social Security Number 999-99-9999, who was receiving home relief based on his application statement that he had no other income, could be identified as the same Charlie Jones, Social Security Number 999-99-9999, who was earning $250 a week as an office clerk. An investigation would then be initiated, and Charlie Jones would be called in for an interview to determine if his benefits should be canceled.

According to the OLAP report, however, this system was not cost-effective because too many of the numbers used in the computer match effort were wrong. If the spot check on Charlie Jones, for instance, found that his Social Security number appeared on a payroll, there was a good likelihood that the welfare department's version of the Social Security number was wrong. Often such numbers had been totally miscopied from the files, or some digits had been transposed. In such cases the welfare recipient turned out not to be the same person as the wage earner.

As a result, many of the investigations and interviews initiated after matching numbers were found were a waste of time. The false matches were costing a lot of money. However, as the department's bookkeeping did not identify all this wasted time as a cost, there was no way to gauge how cost-inefficient the system was. Most likely, though, the money spent tracking down these false matches was greater than any savings realized from catching the small number of welfare cheats through the true matches.

Without a document such as this OLAP report, we could never have challenged the welfare department. Not only was the department too large for an outsider to understand thoroughly, but the policy of protecting the privacy of clients prevented our digging into departmental files. Sources supplying us with internal welfare department information were therefore essential to this investigation.

On May 11 we put out a press release headlined "Social Security Check on Welfare Fraud a Flop." The *Daily News* carried a miniature one-sentence story the next morning. The *Post*, an afternoon paper, called me to ask whether there was some special angle to the story it could use to avoid simply echoing the *News*. I remembered another finding in the OLAP report that we had neglected to mention in our press release—that 22 percent of the welfare case files called for could not be located. That angle became a six-column *Post* headline on page 5.

In releasing information critical of a government agency, we occasionally were pleasantly surprised to find the officials in charge eager to correct deficiencies. More often, of course, the reaction was negative and defensive. This time, though, we were taken aback by the vehemence of the welfare administrator's response.

The welfare administrator—or more formally, administrator of the city's Human Resources Administration (HRA)—was Blanche Bernstein. She had a reputation for being tough on welfare cheats and other abusers of programs for the poor. Those of us who had fought against the empires exploiting poverty programs had therefore applauded her appointment five months earlier.

However, not everyone agreed. From the beginning, Bernstein's appointment had been harshly criticized by the black community, which accused her of firing high-level black employees and retaining high-level white employees. Our welfare department sources, attempting to change our favorable impressions of Bernstein, agreed with us that the blacks she had fired were incompetent. But, they contended, the whites she had retained were incompetent, too. Unfortunately our sources were unable to supply documentary evidence. A clue that we might be wrong and our welfare sources might be right about how good an administrator she would be came in her reaction to our press release.

Bernstein reacted furiously. She put out a ferociously counterattacking press release. Within the space of four pages she called our charges "deplorable," "precipitous," "misleading," "destructive," "erroneous," and "invalid." She called the material in the OLAP report, and therefore in our press release, "erroneous in both preparation and presentation."

This touched off a debate within the welfare department between the authors of the report at OLAP, who defended their assertions, and the upper management. The latter had been assuring Bernstein, still new in the job, that nothing was seriously wrong.

Some of our knowledge of this debate came from an internal memorandum from Bernstein's top deputy. Unfortunately the sources who supplied us with a copy of this memorandum were too frightened of discovery to permit us to release it. They feared it could be traced to them. In the memo the deputy was apparently attempting to conciliate OLAP by conceding some key points.

On the subject of erroneous Social Security numbers, the deputy's memo admitted, "We do make some clerical errors in collecting and transmitting SSN's [Social Security numbers] to the computer file. . . . We would get more 'hits' through our match program if all the SSN's on the file were validated. . . ."

On the subject of the many missing client files, it was interesting that Bernstein was apparently misinformed by her own department. Bernstein had said in her press release that the OLAP study "altogether overlooked the fact that welfare files are not static. Twenty percent or more can be in active use and out of their cabinets for two or three days at a time." The fact was that OLAP reported files as missing only after several *weeks* of search requests. Bernstein's deputy, who had several years of experience in the department and surely knew this, therefore worded his memorandum less combatively: "As many as 10–20% of the case records may not be easily locatable when they are requested because they are in use."

Although we were anxious for the issues of Social Security numbers and missing files to be resolved, we could not substantiate our earlier press release by divulging the deputy's memo because this would have endangered our sources.

For more than two months we were at a standstill. Then we were reminded that a prominent accounting firm had been engaged by the city to audit the HRA. This audit was to be released only to "the client"—i.e., designated city officials—so we were unable to obtain a copy. Instead, I managed to contact by telephone an auditor who had worked on the audit and was willing to talk with me in confidence about its findings.

The auditor was nervous. Nevertheless, he was relieved to talk because he believed his most critical findings were being excised from the audit by his superiors. External auditors occasionally admit that they sometimes pull their punches; clients like city governments with lucrative contracts may not be favorably disposed to award subsequent contracts to auditors who provide harsh and critical audits, particularly because the contents of those audits must eventually become public.

The auditor said, among other devastating comments: (1) Because HRA did not check the Social Security numbers of applicants against those of recipients already on the rolls, the same individual could open cases at two different welfare centers. As long as he/she provided different addresses (not particularly difficult to do), the recipient would not be caught for at least a few months and perhaps longer. This was true even if he/she used the same name and Social Security number at each center. (2) Although a monthly checklist of duplicate names and Social Security numbers was made by HRA, no effective follow-up was used to eliminate the duplicates found. (3) HRA didn't know how many cases were open (receiving assistance). This was because certain efforts to close cases (terminate assistance) were rejected by the computers as a result of programming flaws, even though management recorded the cases as closed.

At the time there was little we could do with the auditor's charges because they were anonymous and made to us by telephone rather than in writing. (For the most part we were unable to document them even when we finally got a copy of the official audit, more than a year later.) We therefore pressed our sources in HRA to come through with hard evidence to support some of the auditor's claims.

Thus, we regarded with awe the enormous stack of computer printouts that we found in a garbage pail—the one next to my desk—placed there, of course, by our usual sources. These, listing welfare clients by name, address, and Social Security numbers, provided us with evidence of inefficiency in regard to Social Security numbers. If the welfare system's computer matching efforts were as effective and sophisticated as the administrator claimed, no two recipients of welfare should have had the same Social Security number because that fact would have turned up in the simplest match of all. Furthermore, no recipients should have lacked Social Security numbers altogether because no checks against them would have been possible; they would have had nothing to match.

Yet what we found when we analyzed the printouts was that 8,000 individuals were receiving welfare on duplicate Social Security numbers. A few recipients even had triplicate numbers. Also listed was a 10,000-name sample of 61,000 total recipients whose case files showed no Social Security numbers at all.

We felt this set of revelations was worth a press conference. We wanted to emphasize that this was not just another welfare fraud story, the typical one of a recipient with a gold Cadillac and fur coat, the one-in-a-thousand case that gives all recipients a bad name. Rather, this evidence pointed to the ineptitude of the system's much-vaunted antifraud techniques.

We solved our concern for the privacy of recipients by eliminating names and addresses from materials we supplied to reporters. We showed the reporters the names and addresses *en masse* on the original printouts, but so quickly that they could not copy any individual names. After all, there was no evidence that any individual on these lists was dishonest. The duplicate or missing numbers could easily have resulted from HRA error. Rather, we stressed that the significance of the printouts was that these were the cases among which fraud was most likely to be prevalent, yet the department's matching efforts were directed against three-quarters of a million recipients who were more straightforward in presenting their Social Security numbers.

On August 4, the day after our press conference, we read the news coverage of our charges. Disappointingly, much space was given to the welfare department's rebuttal, this time from Bernstein's deputy. Our press release had said, "If past patterns are any indication, HRA will denounce my new criticism and will call these revelations 'deplorable.' But we want the facts. . . ." The deputy avoided the word "deplorable"—his choice of adjectives was "disgraceful and irresponsible."

He tried to explain away recipients without numbers by pointing to delays at the Social Security Administration in Washington of up to three months in the processing of applications for Social Security numbers. In other words, Washington was to blame for recipients who had no numbers.

To explain away recipients with duplicate numbers, he said that HRA did a computer search every month to pick up duplicate Social Security numbers; "there are rarely more than a handful outstanding at one time." His explanations appeared to satisfy the newspapers. Reporters did not require him to explain why most of the names on our printout had been receiving welfare for several years.

Although the newspaper reporters had not asked the tough questions of HRA, the questions they had asked apparently sent HRA into an uproar anyway. This new uproar dwarfed the internal debate between OLAP and welfare's upper management following our May press release. After our first release, our sources told us, Bernstein had demanded an internal department investigation to discover who had leaked the draft OLAP report to us. Apparently this took precedence over analyzing our criticism to see if her department's methods might be improved. Now she again seemed to disregard our charges and, instead, demanded a redoubling of efforts to find the leak. Two investigators came to my office and threatened me with court action if I refused to name my sources. When I explained to them that I'd be delighted to address the issue in court, with all sorts of possibilities for new publicity attendant upon such an occasion, they wilted quickly.

Next, Bernstein sent a welfare official to me to pick up the computer printout we had obtained. The pretext was that HRA was interested in addressing the problems we had raised and wanted the printout for information. I explained that since the printout came from HRA computers, HRA could easily replicate it. Bernstein's real purpose in wanting our copy appears to have been less innocent: Certain paper and printing characteristics of a printout can sometimes be used to determine the computer terminal which printed it. Having our copy of the printout might have helped identify the source of the leak.

After failing to obtain the printout from me, HRA had a deputy administrator write a letter to our subcommittee chairman requesting the printout: "You certainly share with us the federal and state requirements as well as the ethical imperative to protect the confidentiality of people receiving welfare grants. In light of your responsibility and ours we wish the return of those names immediately."

Suspecting HRA's true motive for attempting to recapture the printout, I took much pleasure in responding, "No copies of the names and addresses on the computer printout were made, and we will destroy the original printout. Therefore, you can rest easy in the knowledge that there will be no breach of welfare recipients' confidentiality. Best regards."

At about this time a *New York Times* reporter, Myron Farber, was jailed for refusing to reveal his sources in connection with a well-publicized murder trial. On July 25 the *Times* had run an editorial in support of Farber's principled stand. We sent the following letter to the editor, which the *Times* printed on August 9:

As an investigation subcommittee heavily dependent on confidential sources in our efforts to expose and correct government wrongdoing, we strongly sympathize with the views expressed in your July 25 editorial, "The Times in the Dock."

In our experience, inside informants are impelled by conscience to come forward in confidence but are deterred by fear of retribution from speaking publicly. If we were required to reveal their identities, we soon would have no informers. And the kinds of waste and mismanagement we have been able to expose would all have continued unabated, never brought to our attention or to the attention of the public.

Recently, we too were threatened with court action by a city agency for our refusal to reveal the names of our sources within that agency. Instead of addressing its real and unresolved problems, the agency was focusing its attention on efforts to find—and presumably revenge itself upon—the whistle-blowers.

The public should demand protection for those who

protect the public against the efforts of government to hide wrongdoing. The right of newspaper reporters, and all other watchdogs against government abuse, to protect their sources should be cherished by the public, for it is the public whose interests are really under attack.

The *Times* included a sketch of a person blowing a whistle and crouching behind a shield full of arrows that had been shot at him. We presented framed copies of the letter and the sketch, autographed by our subcommittee chairman, to our sources at HRA.

Despite the stories we heard of Bernstein's Queeglike efforts to find the leak, she never did find out who our sources were. Instead, in March 1979, our sources showed me an amazing eight-page report on the unsuccessful eight-month search for the leak. I got a great deal of pleasure reading about all the false trails HRA had followed to end up without any firm conclusion. Our sources were definitively cleared of suspicion.

Our success in protecting our sources was gratifying, but we were still getting nowhere with welfare.

After our August 3 press conference the mayor asked to meet with us. He asked why we had attacked his administration publicly rather than come to him with our problems, given the good working relationship we had had. We said that he had used public criticism as an effective tool of reform before he became mayor; why shouldn't we use it now? He joked back, disarmingly, "But those were the bad guys!"

The mayor had said on previous occasions that Bernstein was his favorite administrator. Now he said to us, soberly, that he had great respect for the way she was standing up to criticism, which included nightly picketing of her house by members of the black community. The mayor's understanding of Bernstein was where ours had been six months earlier, and we endeavored to explain to him what we had learned.

Since many of the matters involved were technical, he suggested that we draft a set of questions which he would require her to answer. We thought that was a fair and sensible idea, and we did it. Among our questions were several concerning the status of the OLAP report. Bernstein had attacked the version we had released in May as merely an early draft full of errors. Now we asked what conclusions were reached in the final report, if it was ready, and how those conclusions differed from the early draft.

In October the mayor gave us a copy of Bernstein's response. It was a lengthy, mealymouthed nondenial of our charges. With respect to the OLAP report, she wrote that it was still in revision, but that HRA had taken "a number of steps to overcome" the problems it had raised.

Our sources told us a different story. They said that only because of the constant pressure we were applying was HRA permitting OLAP to do a final report at all. Even at that, its authors were regularly pressed to tone down, modify, and alter their findings. However, the OLAP authors resisted. On December 28 they completed their work and so informed us. We then began our campaign to get a copy of the final report.

HRA's public relations office stalled and stalled and finally announced that we could have a copy. When we received it, in early February 1979, it was not OLAP's December 28 report. What we got was a later January version by HRA's management, purportedly "based on" the OLAP report. This later version, of course, left out the most critical and important points of the OLAP study.

We had to start all over again to try to get the right report. By late February we had given up on a direct approach to HRA and went back to the mayor's office. A mayoral assistant told us that he would ask for the report on our behalf; after several weeks he, too, was given the January bowdlerized edition. We instructed him to ask more specifically for the December 28 version, and he did so. By the end of March we still did not have it. However, something else had happened by then: Blanche Bernstein had been fired.

The mayor didn't fire her directly. Rather, he appointed Stanley Brezenoff, who had done a magnificent job as commissioner of employment, operating head of HRA and gave Bernstein the undignified option of remaining as nominal head of the agency. Bernstein declined and resigned, and Brezenoff became her successor.

The mayoral assistant told us that her removal had been precipitated by her response to his request for the December

28 OLAP study: she refused to give it to him, although he had asked on behalf of the mayor. (The assistant later denied this story to newspaper reporters. The public explanation of Bernstein's removal was never made more explicit than "management problems.")

We later learned from our sources in HRA and elsewhere that Bernstein might not have been able to supply a copy of the December 28 report even if she had wanted to: a high-ranking HRA official whose identity we never learned had ordered all copies of the report destroyed. But we knew at least two remained.

In April we began requesting a copy from Brezenoff, and he sent it in mid-May. As it happened, he sent it a day after our sources decided it was safe to supply us with their own personal copy. Now we had two.

Brezenoff had sent a four-page cover letter with his, saying that the matter was a "tempest in a teapot." The letter, obviously drafted by someone far more familiar with technical computer issues than Brezenoff could have been after a few weeks in the job, entirely ignored the matter of the missing case files.

The early draft OLAP report—the one that had been thrown over our partition and started us on this case—had argued that HRA could combat fraud more effectively by targeting for investigation certain types of cases, including those without files. The statistical likelihood of fraud among those cases was higher. Specific recommendations for such targeting had appeared in both the May and the December drafts, but Bernstein had apparently been too busy looking for leaks and attempting to suppress the report to implement any of its recommendations.

But in the December 28 report OLAP had added a bombshell to the initial findings: Statistics showed a connection between missing case files and welfare clients who failed to appear when called in for interviews.

OLAP had taken two random samples of welfare recipients from among those whose Social Security number records were characterized by some type of discrepancy—usually more than one number recorded at various places for the same recipient. One sample was of recipients for whom files could be located in welfare centers; the other was of recipients for whom files could not be found. Names and addresses of recipients whose files were missing were obtained from the HRA computer list for mailing the checks and the federal Social Security number records. Welfare clients in both samples were called in for interviews. Some in each sample failed to come in, but a far higher percentage of those without files failed to come in.

The OLAP report showed a statistical probability of 0.999997 that there was a positive relationship between the 14 percent of the active case files that could not be found (as against 22 percent of all case files, active or inactive) and clients who failed to appear for interviews. That is, a person receiving a welfare check whose case record could not be found was much less likely to show up when the department called him or her in for an interview.

This strange statistical correlation raised many questions. How could a client know that the department couldn't find his/her record? Was it possible that missing records were those of ineligible welfare recipients? Was there collusion between welfare department personnel and ineligible recipients? In fact, if the case record was missing and the client failed to show up for an interview, was the client just a name in the computer? Was such a client nonexistent?

Fraud was a possibility. Certain clerks—perhaps the head control clerks in welfare centers—could put a case into the computer records without a case file. These clerks could arrange to have welfare checks made out to anyone—either someone who would kick back money to the clerk or a fictitious person whose check would be cashed in some way by the clerk.

All check recipients were called in for recertification every three months, and many thousands of recipients didn't come. They were then removed from the rolls, but 70 percent were back on the rolls, often for valid reasons, within two or three months. However, fake cases could be returned to the rolls the same way. Numerous cases were closed voluntarily, just before recertification, every three months. These, too, could be fake cases. With no case file to trigger suspicion, the fake would be harder to find.

Since 14 percent of the active case files were missing, even a small percentage of that number involved in fraud would represent many millions of dollars of fraud annually.

Of course, such possibilities were part of the price of modern technology. None of this could have happened in the days when each recipient had his/her own caseworker assigned by the welfare department. At that time ineligibility among recipients was about 2 percent. With computerization and the end of that system, caseworkers came into contact with only a small minority of clients, and the department now admitted to an ineligibility rate of about 9 percent. Thus far, however, it would not admit to the vulnerability of this system to large-scale fraud perpetrated by its own employees creating fictitious cases.

The question we faced in late May was whether to make public the information that HRA was suppressing a report critical of its operations, that the department's systems were vulnerable to fraud, and that such fraud could cost the city millions of dollars annually.

Our conclusion was that a public exposé would be premature and unfair. For one thing, if fraud did exist, an exposé would be likely to scare off any culprits before we could make a solid case against them. Then, too, apart from the strange statistic, we had no evidence of fraud. Perhaps we, our sources, and OLAP were somehow missing valid alternative explanations for the statistical relationship. Perhaps no fictitious cases or collusion existed at all. Much more work—work that required cooperation from insiders at welfare—remained to be done before we could go public.

Although we did further work, including questioning our sources, we failed to obtain evidence of fraud. We did learn that OLAP had tried to examine the relationship between missing files and no-show clients by initiating a small follow-up study. This study was a sample of seventeen clients whose files were missing and who had failed to respond to an interview request. Investigators went to the addresses listed for the seventeen and questioned landlords, superintendents, fellow tenants, and neighbors about these welfare clients. The experienced investigators were able to overcome and discount for the natural reluctance of people in poor neighborhoods to disclose such information. In sixteen of the seventeen cases, no one had ever seen or heard of the recipient during the time that the recipient was supposedly receiving welfare checks at that address. Nevertheless, those checks were being cashed. Unfortunately, although we were told that a memorandum on these findings had been sent to OLAP, we were unable to get a copy either from our sources at OLAP or from the investigators who had made the study.

Next, I called friends in the Social Services Employees Union, whose members work for the welfare department. I thought that the surreptitious and confidential use of union people employed at good vantage points would help us track down nonexistent welfare recipients. If the check never came back from the address of a nonresident recipient, we would have narrowed our suspicions to the mail carrier or other residents at the address. On the other hand, if the check were returned, union people could track its course in the bureaucracy to see if it had stuck to someone's hands along the route. Undeliverable checks were eventually supposed to be validated and then sent to the recipient's welfare center to be picked up by the recipient. Union employees could monitor that end, too, to see who eventually picked up the check.

But our union contacts could not obtain a sample of nonresident recipients. Without this, we were stalled. Our only chance now was to enlist Brezenoff's help. His inexperience could excuse his "tempest in a teapot" letter to us. Obviously he had relied on his aides to explain a computer problem he understood no better than we did. Our job was to try to convince him that someone other than his self-interested aides should investigate our charges. Thus, a meeting we set up with Brezenoff for July 2 was critical.

Brezenoff, not surprisingly, was not alone. With him were five aides. One of these was the deputy who had stonewalled us during Bernstein's tenure. Another was the man who had written the bowdlerized January version of the OLAP report. Brezenoff, apparently briefed by aides, got the meeting off to an unpromising start by reiterating some of the points of his May 14 letter to us. We quickly steered the meeting onto the subject of the relationship between the missing files and the failure of clients to appear at interviews.

Brezenoff was patently astonished. He asked us if that

problem had been mentioned in the OLAP report. Obviously he had not seen it, and his aides had failed to bring it to his attention. I showed him the discussion in the December report and told him how it had been left out of the January version. Brezenoff then asked his aides what had been done after this problem had been raised by OLAP. Their answers were so vague and confusing that Brezenoff said, "This is a nightmare!"

At long last we had an administrator of HRA who was willing to listen. I explained our theory of fictitious cases created with the internal collusion of HRA employees, and our subcommittee chairman asked Brezenoff's aides to provide an alternative explanation. They could not, but one aide did try to explain why our theory was impossible. He did not convince anyone.

Next, we discussed the missing files. At first the stonewalling deputy tried to use his old excuse that the files could not be found because they were in use. Finally, Brezenoff asked him what percentage of the files could be retrieved after every avenue of search was explored and all necessary time was allowed. While the deputy's response of 88 percent seemed high to us, it was a first admission that a sizable portion of the files could never be found.

When Brezenoff asked us what we recommended, we proposed the outlines of the investigation we had initially worked out with the union. Brezenoff said that he would ask the investigations department to set up the inquiry under an investigator whose reputation was excellent. We left the meeting well satisfied. We thought this assured that the investigation would be handled with competence and integrity. On July 26, with the investigations department, we plotted the course of the study, fleshing out some of the points we had outlined with Brezenoff. On August 22 copies of the formal work plan were sent to Brezenoff, our subcommittee chairman, and me.

Although this sounded like a good start, we were warned that a full inquiry would take months. It did.

On February 7 of the following year the subcommittee chairman and I were called in to be briefed by Brezenoff and HRA officials on the investigations department findings. We were solemnly told that the inquiry had corroborated that a statistical relationship existed between missing files and no-shows at call-in. The Alice in Wonderland world of the welfare department reasserted itself with the further news that it had no hypothesis to explain the statistics.

In the months since our last meeting, and after considerable expenditure of investigative time, all welfare had done was to replicate OLAP's year-old findings. At least HRA was no longer denying that the statistical correlation existed. But although it had no better theory than our suggestion of collusion, it denied that collusion existed because the investigations department had failed to turn up evidence of fraud.

Well, the search for a satisfactory explanation was to continue, and we were advised to check back in a few weeks. Eventually the investigations department examiner got a new job and left the case. A new irritant was that in some cases in which the investigations department wanted to locate questionable clients, it asked HRA to continue sending checks so their route could be traced. HRA ignored this request and closed the cases, making tracing impossible. In our subsequent attempts to follow up, we were told that most of the missing files had been located. We were also told that most of the no-shows at interviews were actual people, not fictitious clients. We had no way of knowing whether any of this was true.

In the end we had made some minor reforms. A stonewalling administrator had been replaced by one willing to be more publicly accountable. We had won a victory for the confidentiality of our sources. Our pressure had made welfare look around for a lot of missing files and keep its records in better order. And the department claimed to have solved some of its computer programing problems so that it was no longer possible for recipients to sign up at several centers for duplicate benefits.

Yet I felt defeated. Our accomplishments paled against the enormousness of what seemed to be a haywire department where new clues led only to new mysteries. What with departmental secrecy, computer technology, and the sheer size and complexity of HRA, we had never been in full control of this investigation.

What's more, I felt that huge departments such as welfare could easily veer out of the control even of their own officials.

Computerization simply complicated an already tangled skein. Unable to compete with the private sector for technical specialists, governmental agencies ran a high risk in trying to accommodate new technology with inept personnel. The growth of government agencies and the rapid changeableness of technology will in the future pose unique problems for administrators and reformers alike.

15

Pyrrhic Victory

IN *The Abuse of Power,* Jack Newfield and Paul DuBrul note that among the biggest contributors to Abraham Beame's 1973 mayoral campaign were real estate operators Charles Bassine, Harry Helmsley, Irving Schneider, Samuel Rudin, Charles Sigety, Sigmund Sommer, and Sheldon Solow, who together contributed more than $100,000, which is a lot in a mayoral campaign. Furthermore, Abraham "Bunny" Lindenbaum, "lawyer and lobbyist for most of the big landlords," was one of Beame's "best and oldest friends." In 1976 Lindenbaum received a $35,000 brokerage fee from the city in connection with the sale of city property to real estate developer Charles Benenson. Benenson paid $2 million for the property; the original asking price had been $3 million. Lindenbaum was paid *by the city,* it seems, for getting the city to accept $1 million less than its asking price.

Real estate is a key element in the web of influence in city government. Hidden behind a technical language of words like "abatements," "amortization," "in rem," "certiorari," and "Section Eight" are some of the most lucrative deals in the public sector—deals that enrich real estate operators at the expense of the public.

It was well known in 1977 that the big real estate operators in New York City had excellent relations with City Hall. To a reformer, these operators represented an irresistible investigative target. They were not ignorant street thugs bought off with one federally funded antipoverty program or another;

177

these were well-educated, well-connected, well-lawyered pillars of the establishment. They didn't break the laws. They had the legislators rewrite the laws. Their money-making schemes did not become scandals; they became matters of public debate, with the public finally uncertain whether the projects were in the public interest.

In June 1976 a city councilman released a report on city leasing practices, in which he charged that the city paid too much rent for much of the space it leased and that many of its leases were held by major political contributors. He listed landlords for the city in Manhattan who had contributed to Beame's mayoral race but took pains to note "in no way is this information meant to imply that they received their leases because of their contributions. In fact, the vast majority of these leases were signed during previous administrations."

On the basis of informal, unofficial, and undocumented allegations that had been made to me, I felt that the councilman's report understated the problem. In fact, I thought it should have been possible to link individual campaign contributors to leases. One huge realty firm, for example, made contributions of thousands of dollars to each of several candidates in the 1977 mayoral primary. Any of several candidates, had they won, would have "owed" it. I thought we would shortly be able to draft a release saying:

> The Department of Real Estate has responded to questions about a lease that seemed to be very unfair to New York City in charging outrageous rent by saying "———— [a powerful political leader] wanted it"; the city pays rent to another politically connected landlord to occupy six stories of his building, which is only three stories high; landlords owing millions of dollars to the city in back taxes are still receiving millions of dollars from the city in rent.

I first envisioned such a statement in March 1977. We hoped to have documentation by the end of the summer. But we never did.

Much of the case rode on the relationship between the price the landlords had paid for their buildings and the rent the city paid the landlords, even discounting for inflation. The councilman had stated that "in Manhattan alone, city rental payments cover the full purchase price of six leased buildings in one year; of fifteen leased buildings in one to three years; of another six buildings in from three to five years." Surely this was just the tip of the iceberg. Wouldn't we soon be able to make out a much more far-reaching indictment? No. We could not even prove that the councilman's findings really represented serious charges.

What the councilman's report had overlooked was the factor of building alteration costs. Say he had criticized the city for paying $500,000 in one year's rent to a landlord who had purchased the building for $500,000. He might have overlooked the $3 million in alterations the landlord claimed to have put into the building. Thus, our subcommittee's research assistant wrote in her August 1977 memorandum: "While approximately 30 buildings in Manhattan and Brooklyn had purchase price to rent ratios which looked highly questionable, the factor of building alterations by the landlord has made this case nearly impossible to verify . . . the eight or so estimated alterations figures which I have been able to find (in leases or files) have shattered the cases. . . ."

Our researcher found that the files at the real estate department, the city office responsible for keeping track of city leasing, were in disastrous condition. It was extremely difficult to find alterations figures in those files and impossible to find supporting documentation for the figures that could be found.

We could not announce apparently outrageous purchase-price-to-rent ratios and leave ourselves open to refutation by the landlords, who would have access to their own alterations cost figures.

Nor, practically speaking, could we subpoena those figures from them. While we had a theoretical subpoena power, we could exercise it only with the approval of the Assembly speaker; unless we had very solid reason to believe that the figures would show wrongdoing, we could not expect cooperation in instituting such an embarrassing proceeding against anyone, much less these politically connected landlords. Besides, there was no guarantee that the figures they would give us would be correct.

But our researcher found another set of alterations figures in the city's records: in the records of the buildings department. Buildings kept the figures not to gauge appropriate rents that the city would have to pay, but rather to gauge the fee that the landlords would have to pay to the city for their alterations permits. Therefore, just as the landlords had an incentive to submit high figures to the real estate department, they had an incentive to submit low figures to the buildings department.

The juxtaposition of the buildings figures with the few real estate department figures we did have was startling.

In one case, the city was paying Charles Benenson $750,000 a year in rent for a building which he had purchased for $1.5 million, thereby apparently letting him make back his purchase price every two years. Benenson claimed, however, that he had had to put $3 to $4 million in alterations into the building—that is, he claimed $3 to $4 million to the real estate department. To buildings, he claimed $400,000. The difference was that, according to the real estate figure, he was making back his investment every six or seven years. This was a fairly reasonable gross return of 15 percent or so a year, out of which he would have to pay expenses. According to the buildings figure, however, he was making a gross return of almost 40 percent a year, a high level of profit. Benenson had contributed $4,000 to the 1973 Beame campaign.

In another case, the city was paying Seymour Cohen $1 million in rent for a building that he had purchased for $4.5 million. Cohen claimed to real estate that he put in another $2.5 million in alterations, but he told buildings about only $125,000 of them. The difference here was between a gross profit of 20 and 40 percent. Cohen had contributed $6,000 to the 1973 Beame campaign and was collecting a total of $5 million in rent from the city from all his buildings.

In a third case, the city was paying Sol Goldman $140,000 in rent for a building he had purchased for $350,000. Goldman told real estate that his alterations costs were $700,000, but buildings had them recorded as $65,000. Was Goldman grossing 14 percent or 35 percent? This was only one Goldman building. Furthermore, Goldman owed the city more than $18 million in back taxes, and the city was still paying him

$1 million a year in rent (without even deducting a percentage to collect on his debts).

It would have been a powerful exposé had we known that the buildings figures were right and the real estate figures were wrong. But our best information at the time was that the two sets of figures were equally unreliable.

Logically it would seem that the real estate department figures should have been too high. Certainly the big money to be made by the landlords was in inflating the real estate figures because millions of dollars in rent rode on those figures. The buildings figures controlled only a few thousand dollars in alterations fees. But we didn't know. Had we had the personnel or budget, we could have hired a construction cost estimator to examine each building and estimate the cost of the alterations for us; but we did know that the buildings figures were at least somewhat low, so it would have been dangerous to make accusations about high profit margins for landlords based on them.

Finally, we simply asked buildings and real estate to explain the contradictory figures. They passed on our questions to the landlords, who "corrected" the figures they had submitted to buildings.

In January 1978 the New York *Post* reported that as a result of the efforts of our subcommittee, Cohen, Benenson, and Goldman were billed a total of $6,000 in additional alterations permit fees and, from then on, buildings and real estate would cross-check alterations figures submitted to them.

It had very much the feeling of a Pyrrhic victory.

16

Invisible Students

THE POLITICS OF university life is often said to be as tough and vicious as any politics. Unfortunately fraud and dishonesty are not always barred from the hallowed halls of academe either. Our exposé of an overbilling scheme by one of the municipal colleges produced some of the most vicious responses we ever experienced and only the most grudging, reluctant admission and correction of the problem.

In the winter of 1978 I ran into a family friend at a symphony concert. In response to my description of my work, my friend pressed me to investigate what she described as a very corrupt situation at New York City Community College, a branch of the City University and therefore a city government institution.

In subsequent meetings with my friend and other confidential sources she provided in the college's faculty and administration, it was alleged that "ghost" classes were created and assigned to favored instructors, who were usually also administrators, thus enabling them to receive pay for classes they didn't have to teach. The ghost classes were called developmental writing and developmental math laboratories, remedial adjuncts to regular English and mathematics classes. Apparently the practice was to encourage all students to sign up for these classes, whether or not they needed the help. The additional class hours did not cost full-time students any money, but the school—and through it, the instructors—were reimbursed for the classroom hours by the state.

Our sources named individual administrators who were responsible for and benefited from this policy. However, we were unable to document individual benefits because we could not prove which laboratory sections were ghosts and which were real. We were able, however, to document the fake student enrollments.

One document we received was a listing of the number of students enrolled in each section of the remedial writing class; another document gave us the schedule showing the meeting time for the section. All the sections met in one place, the remedial writing laboratory. Thus, we were able to determine that, for example, on Monday afternoon at one o'clock 165 students were registered for the course and on Wednesday at noon 198 students were enrolled.

The problem was that the room in question held only 40.

By adding up the total number of registered students and subtracting the maximum classroom capacity at each hour, we came up with the number of ghost students. In total, 883 more students were assigned to the room than could have squeezed into it. Since the state reimbursement was paid on the basis of $850 per full-time equivalent (FTE) student (15 credits) per semester, we could charge that the college over-billed the state by at least $55,000 per semester for this course alone.

The significance was at least threefold, beyond the problem of overbilling. First, since several different sections, each with its own instructor, were scheduled for the room at any given time, it was easy for an instructor not to attend and let one of the other scheduled instructors take charge that day. However, since we had no records of instructor attendance, we could not prove this charge.

Secondly, we were told that students were instructed to fill out enrollment forms for these classes in such a way that they often did not realize they were enrolled. Our sources gave us the names of students who, not needing remedial help, were surprised when we told them they were enrolled.

Thirdly, sources also gave us transcripts for students who had been graded, often without their knowledge, for the classes in question. For students who hadn't required remedial help, transcripts showing remedial courses could have created serious academic problems in the future.

While sources insisted that the school received reimbursement for these courses from the state, we needed to check that out. We consulted an analyst on the staff of the legislative committee that supervises the City University, who confirmed the story. Since the City University budget was inaccessible, we did not pursue this question further.

We decided simply to call on the city to explain the discrepancies we had noted. We expected this to be sufficiently embarrassing so that the college would end these dishonest practices.

On May 23, 1978, the chairman of the subcommittee and I, accompanied by newspaper reporters and a CBS-TV camera crew and reporter, visited the remedial writing laboratory, where 2 of 3 assigned instructors and 17 of 113 registered students were in attendance.

At first the press conference went well. Only 17 students were in attendance; our press release figures had given the school the benefit of the doubt by allowing for 40. Then the assistant to the president of the college heard we were there and came to the classroom to ask what the problem was. When we explained it to him, he said that the laboratory fell under a special classification which meant it was not reimbursable; therefore, the college received "not one penny" from the state for it.

The president's assistant was steady and cool. The subcommittee chairman asked me how to respond, and I went to telephone the City University committee analyst. The analyst picked this uncomfortable moment to alter his position. Now he said that it was *possible* that the course was not reimbursable.

This was a major crisis. Without a financial irregularity there was no story, and we would lose all credibility with the press. The impact of our presentation would have been dissipated. Even if we were able to reestablish the proof of the charges a few days later, we would not be able to reawaken editors' interest. No reporters would be sent the second time, and no one would ever know we had been right the first time.

The president's assistant invited us into the office of the dean to discuss the charges. A bewildered press corps followed.

By this time I had turned an unhealthy shade of green. The subcommittee chairman later told me he feared I might kill myself. Nonetheless, I began to cross-examine the dean and quickly produced the admission that the course was indeed reimbursed by the state. The sense of relief was unforgettable. The press conference ended on that note—happily for the subcommittee.

The president's assistant had simply lied. Later in the afternoon I got an urgent message to call him. The president's assistant said, "I am calling to tell you as a friend—I was right the first time, and the dean was wrong. To save yourself some embarrassment when this comes out, you'd better call the press and tell them." His effrontery was incredible, but his gamble on our conscientious innocence almost worked.

We felt that we had a hard decision to make since we did not know whether he was lying again. We knew, however, that if we told the press we were uncertain and asked for more time, no one would be willing to write the story. Then the fraud—if it existed—would continue unabated. Since the story involved no accusation against any individual and the only reputations that could be damaged if the story were wrong were our own, we decided to let it run.

The press reported the chancellor of the entire City University system as saying, "Of course, I am not going to do anything about it. There is nothing to do anything about."

The chancellor (or his staff) apparently was not satisfied merely to make this incredible response. Next, on June 9, 1978, a letter appeared in the "Letters to the Editor" column of *The New York Times* excoriating us for our "invasion" of the classroom. The letter was signed "William Birenbaum." We suspected that this was no independent effort but somehow was linked to the college or to the chancellor's office. The latter turned out to have been more likely. A call to the chancellor's office for William Birenbaum produced his wife's office in the financial department. When the secretary was asked why a request for William Birenbaum should produce his wife's office, she replied, "Well, he can be reached here, too," —apparently indicating that he did indeed have a connection to the chancellor's office and adding to our suspicion that his letter was not merely that of a "concerned citizen."

Birenbaum's outrageous letter read as follows:

To the Editor:

The unauthorized invasions of a New York City Community College classroom on May 28 [sic—it was the twenty-third] by State Assemblyman Charles E. Schumer, Chairman of the Assembly's Subcommittee on City Management, is a dangerous and inexcusable breach of academic freedom.

He alleged that officials of that college are spending public funds improperly. That allegation may be pursued through the orderly processes of government, which Mr. Schumer is bound by oath to uphold.

The threshold of a classroom is sacred, and many in higher education have fought long and hard to resist the invasion of the classroom by C.I.A. and F.B.I. agents and others who have tried to intimidate those inside.

Mr. Schumer's unanounced appearance with a retinue of TV and press reporters was a cheap political shot, demeaning of the democratic institutions he especially should uphold in the presence of the younger.

If the administration of that college is abusing its budget, neither the teacher nor the students in the classroom are liable. To get his few inches in your paper, Mr. Schumer has done great damage to a principle of much greater value than any fraud which may be involved.

William Birenbaum, May 28, 1978

This absurd letter, either shockingly stupid or else obviously disingenuous inasmuch as Birenbaum was a college president himself (first of a City University branch on Staten Island and later of Antioch), proved useful. It gave us an excellent opportunity to rebut one line of attack and to place in the public record a statement of our operating principles. On June 24 our response appeared in the same column:

To the Editor:

Since the issue raised by William Birenbaum in his

June 9 letter to the Times on Assemblyman Schumer's classroom "invasion" appeared in different guises in the past, I think it is time to provide a public airing of the problem.

The Times reported Assemblyman Schumer's disclosures that New York City Community College claimed state reimbursement for hundreds of students supposedly enrolled in a course who did not know they were enrolled, who never attended and whose attendance was not even physically possible. The dean of the college, in the same article, admitted the charges. Nonetheless, Mr. Birenbaum called our presentation of these disclosures at the college "a dangerous and inexcusable breach of academic freedom." Since Schumer's revelations were hardly the sort that could intimidate those inside the classroom, and had no bearing on the subject of instruction—which the assemblyman praised—the charge of breaching academic freedom is obviously silly.

Nevertheless, Birenbaum's letter does touch on a real issue—the *public* exposure of problems of this sort, as opposed to persevering through other channels.

An assemblyman like Schumer, unless he has a key legislative position such as Speaker, has rather limited power. Initially, when Schumer found problems in government, he would call or write to the government official in charge, and usually get promises of action. Later, when he would check to see what happened, he usually received lame excuses about why solutions could not be effected. In the end, nothing happened.

In the past few years, however, Schumer has adopted the view that public airing of these problems is a better approach. In this manner, our subcommittee's work has resulted in the termination of several fraudulent drug-abuse treatment programs, the reduction of city asphalt purchasing costs by about $1.5 million, the reform of the city's auction process, and the emergency allocation of $1 million in funding to a city hospital where patients are dying because of nursing shortages. We have found that when the public media report this kind of problem, solutions are somehow found much more quickly. In the deservedly much-quoted phrase of Justice Brandeis, "Sunlight is the best disinfectant."

At stake indeed is "a principle of much greater value than any fraud which may be involved" at New York City Community College, but Mr. Birenbaum's notions are a perversion of that principle. The principle is the free exchange of ideas and information, the *sine qua non* of democratic government.

Daniel Feldman, Counsel, Assembly Subcommittee
on City Management, June 9, 1978

Meanwhile, we were attempting to elicit from the chancellor of the City University system a response to the specific questions we had raised: What was the extent of overbilling, and what would be done about it? First, we wrote to him asking him to explain his purported remark that "there was nothing to do anything about." He replied that he believed his comment "was to the effect that if the College's explanation of the open lab was correct then there was nothing to do anything about," and he pledged to investigate all charges.

On July 7 we wrote to him again, asking him to expand his inquiry to other remedial classes and also asking for copies of the grade sheets for the courses we had questioned. (We had been alerted to the fact that grades of W were entered for students who had not attended.) On August 8 the chancellor responded that our request "perplexed" him and asked us to explain it. On August 11 we did so, and the chancellor once again promised to look into it.

Later in August the chancellor's assistant called to say that "the problem has been resolved"—with no further details. Since we did not feel very reassured, we demanded specifics. Grudgingly the chancellor's assistant agreed to send a detailed written response.

On September 7 the chancellor's assistant wrote to us that "a total of 560 average annualized full-time equivalent (FTE) students who would have been associated with all three open labs (reading, mathematics, and writing) have [sic] been excluded from the official enrollment of New York City Community College." This represented almost $1 million in billings, much more than our original investigation had revealed. In addition, as a result of this investigation of abuse of remedial labs, he wrote that "the College has found it necessary to suspend operation of these labs for 1978–79" and that they would be reopened the following year only on condition that no state reimbursement be sought. This would certainly prevent their abuse by favored faculty to get compensation for courses not taught, although we had never made that point explicit.

Ironically, the following September the state comptroller issued an audit on state financial assistance to the City University community colleges, disallowing reimbursement for 201 FTE students—a total of $148,740 claimed for remedial laboratories at New York City Community College. The audit noted that many students were automatically and involuntarily registered for the labs and that they received passing grades even if they never attended. But the comptroller's audit and disallowance were based on the fiscal year ended June 1975! Had we waited for official channels to resolve the problem as it existed in 1978, we probably would have had to wait until at least 1982.

We learned several lessons in this battle. One, university bureaucrats fight as dirty and can be just as bad as any other kind. Two, a canny bureaucrat may understand that a well-placed brazen lie can save him a lot of trouble, and we must be prepared to face that kind of response with better documentation. Three, without follow-up, the fruits of all previous efforts can easily be lost.

17

Going, Going, Gone

WE HELD OUR press conference in front of a horrible slum building. We had picked a particularly graphic example for maximum media coverage and impact on the public and thus indirectly on the administration.

The building, 457 West 125th Street in Harlem, had forty-nine individual violations, including vermin, roaches, defective fire escape, no hot water, falling plaster, and leaking ceilings. The family who owned it obviously failed to maintain it. They also had failed to pay taxes on it, and they owed the city at least $140,000 in back taxes.

Eventually the city would take the building over for non-payment of taxes. In the meantime, however, the family had just bought seven more buildings at the auction of city-held property.

The story of the subcommittee's battle to reform the city's real estate auction process provides an excellent model of the successful application of reform techniques. Although the exploiters of the old auction system were not as wealthy or powerful as the landlords who defeated us in the city leasing battle, the problems the auction exploiters were causing the city were probably even more serious.

There were many reasons for the deterioration of urban neighborhoods in the 1960's and 1970's. Each reason, by itself, constituted a major threat to the city's well-being. One was the destructive "milking," by which landlords collected rent from tenants but did nothing to maintain the buildings, until the buildings finally deteriorated to the point of uninhabitability.

In many cases, particularly with the rise in heating oil prices in the mid-1970's, landlords were caught between maintenance costs and rent control, meaning that they could not increase rents enough to cover costs. These landlords simply could not maintain their buildings. In other cases, neighborhoods were so bad that reliable rent-paying tenants could not be found for them. These buildings could not be maintained either.

Unfortunately marginal buildings which could have been saved with proper management were often the victims of unscrupulous landlords, and as a result, marginal neighborhoods which could have been improved were instead ruined.

One of the unmistakable characteristics of a building being milked was the failure of its landlord to pay real estate taxes. The city's Housing Development Administration found an almost perfect statistical correlation between tax arrears on the one hand and violations, disrepair, and abandonment on the other.

The city had a method for dealing with landlords who didn't pay their real property taxes. After three years of failure to pay, the city could take the property in rem—that is, in lieu of the taxes owed. Then the property would be put up for sale at periodic auctions of surplus city-owned real estate; on being sold to a new owner who would pay taxes, the property went back on the active tax rolls as a generator of revenue for the city.

As it happened, however, the theory of the auction process all too frequently failed to be reflected in reality. In March 1977 the subcommittee chairman was given a copy of a study of the tax foreclosure and auction process. The study, completed by the city's Housing Development Administration in December 1975, had never before been released. The author of the study, long frustrated by the city's failure to act on its findings, had finally come to us for action.

The study was called "Real Estate Tax Patterns of Multiple Dwellings Taken by the City for Non-Payment of Taxes and

Resold from January, 1972 to December, 1974." It showed that certain speculators would buy city property at auction and collect rent, but pay no real estate taxes and provide no services or maintenance. Eventually the city would foreclose on the property and then sell it again at auction. But the speculator could usually count on holding the building for at least four years (not the statutory three years) before the city could arrange to take it in rem.

Then the speculator would return to the city auction, when the property was to be resold, buy back the same property under a different name or another property—often for no more than a fraction of the unpaid taxes—and once again refuse to pay the taxes or maintain the building.

Of 166 randomly chosen auction properties the study surveyed, 94 percent were in tax arrears again within four years or less, and 97 percent of those which were occupied had reported violations. For 60 percent, *no* taxes had been paid since resale, and more than 50 percent had thirty or more violations. The study concluded that many bidders must have made their purchases *intending* not to pay the taxes they would incur.

According to one city official, the real property tax losses to the city in this manner had amounted to more than half a billion dollars in uncollected taxes since 1967; the damage done to the city's housing stock was immeasurable.

A minor but commendable effort to remedy the situation was made by a city councilman who pushed through a local law in 1976 that enabled the city to take property in rem after one year of tax arrears instead of three. But just as the landlords had been able to hold the buildings for four years instead of three because of bureaucratic time lags, even under the new law the tax-delinquent landlords got more than two years to milk the buildings they had purchased.

The auction system favored buyers with bad intentions. There was certainly less short-term profit to a landlord who intended to do an honest job of rehabilitating a marginal building than to one who intended to milk it and run. Thus, a bidder not planning to pay for repairs or meet tax obligations could bid higher than a bidder with honest intentions since he/she could project a higher cash return from the building.

When our subcommittee was formed, one of its first jobs was to determine whether the results of the Housing Development Administration report were still valid. We selected twenty-five buildings at random from those auctioned off by the city from December 1975 through March 1976. For eight of the buildings, title never passed—for one reason or another, the auction purchaser never completed the transaction. For three, some taxes had been paid. For fourteen, no taxes had been paid. Obviously the problem still existed.

In the course of updating the study, we came across one purchaser who had bought at least fourteen buildings from the city between 1974 and 1976, all of which were still in arrears. This buyer had bought additional properties, although he refused to pay taxes on properties he already owned. His example more or less scotched the argument that auction purchasers were merely the victims of rent control and high fuel costs. If owning these marginal properties was such a painful economic ordeal, why buy more of them?

On March 11, 1977, our chairman released the original Housing Development Administration study and the subcommittee update. The New York *Post* and the *Times* carried the story, but not prominently. The *Times* also carried the response of the city's real estate department, which supervised the auctions. The department said that by law tax-foreclosed properties were sold at auction to the highest bidders—period.

Obviously we had to do something else to attract real estate's attention if we wanted improvements.

I decided that we could sue the city to force the real estate department to stop selling property to tax-delinquent landlords. The legal theory would be based on some responsibility the municipality must have to protect its own financial interests on behalf of its taxpayers. Once we could locate such a legal duty, we would show that, by failing to exclude tax-delinquent speculators from the auctions, the city was being derelict in that duty. We would also show that it could legally exclude such speculators from the auctions.

At the auction on March 21, 1977, we served papers on the representative of the real estate department to begin a lawsuit in which we sought a court order to require the city to impose an affidavit requirement on auction bidders. The affidavit we sought would: (1) exclude purchasers who were more than a year in arrears on any property owned, directly or through a corporation or partnership, and (2) bar purchase at auction of a property in which the bidder had previously held an interest.

This event was covered only by the *Daily News*. The *News* concluded the story by reporting that a spokesman for the real estate department "refuted Schumer's contentions by saying that most of the auctioned residential property was bought by people who lived in the buildings rather than renting them out."

This "refutation" taught us two lessons. The first was that, under pressure, city spokespersons would simply lie. The second and more painful lesson was that reporters sometimes wrote their stories without further investigation—as if such lies, as long as they were from official sources, constituted definitive refutations of charges made against the agencies. The agencies, of course, were assumed to have more information than the critics. . . .

This got us mad. Six days later we staged the press conference in front of the slum owned by the family who had just bought seven more buildings at auction. Our press release for this event began:

Assemblyman Charles Schumer said today that a spot-check of those who bought property at the City real estate auction last Tuesday, March 22 turned up several buyers from whom the City has been unable to collect over $175,000 in tax arrears on buildings they already owned. The Assemblyman, who chairs the Subcommittee on City Management, had warned the City of such buyers in public statements on March 11 and at the first auction on Monday, March 21, but according to one newspaper account, the Department of Real Estate "refuted Schumer's contentions by saying that most of the auctioned residential property was bought by people who lived in the buildings rather than renting them out."

In fact, only 2 of the 102 properties sold in Manhattan

and Brooklyn were bought by people who lived in them. At least 41 were bought by purchasers of more than one building each.

The story was covered in the *Times* and the *News* and on several television stations. The city began to realize that it had a fight on its hands and that we were not going to drop the matter after a headline or two.

The city's reluctance to remedy the situation remains truly puzzling. To this day no evidence has surfaced of any corruption or impropriety on the part of the officials who ran the auctions. One can only surmise that the city's inertia may have been an unwillingness to admit error. Perhaps it was especially galling to admit that a young assemblyman might know better than the city's experts on the subject. But after the third press release, we stirred some action. The acting commissioner of real estate, a nonpolitical career civil servant, told the subcommittee that the sale of properties at the March 22 auction, to three successful bidders whose other properties were significantly in tax arrears, would be held up.

After we announced this first step toward success, the acting commissioner was apparently overruled by John Carroll, the head of the Municipal Services Administration. The real estate department was under the Municipal Services Administration, and Carroll was a political appointment of the mayor's. The administration, apparently, was still not ready to concede error to the upstart assemblyman. The story in the *Daily News* on April 12 said that while our chairman had announced that the city had "agreed to take the first step" toward ending the sale of auctioned property to real estate tax scofflaws, "the city department denied that it had ever done so."

We brought in a little more artillery. Our chairman introduced a bill in the Assembly that would have the same effect as our lawsuit: to require the city to demand affidavits from auction bidders affirming that they were not already in default on properties owned. It would certainly look peculiar for the city to oppose this bill in Albany while complaining of its terrible financial condition; what argument was there for gambling away the city's ability to collect real estate taxes?

We introduced the bill partly because we had some questions about the prospects of the lawsuit. The city's papers, in response to those we served, argued, first, that the exclusion of bidders from the auction limited competition, thereby preventing sale at the highest marketable price (a requirement under the City Charter for sale of city property), and, secondly, that our chairman had no legal standing, as an aggrieved party in the legal sense, to bring the suit. (We had added a copetitioner, a neighborhood housing activist who had been discouraged from bidding by the city's auction practices, but the city argued that his legal standing was flimsy, too.)

Our memorandum in opposition noted that sales to known tax delinquents were not sales at the highest marketable price in terms of bringing the highest monetary return to the city. A true accounting would have to consider the future taxes which the city could expect *not* to collect. Therefore, we argued, the city was *obliged* to exclude tax delinquents in order to increase the likelihood of sales at the highest marketable price.

On the question of our chairman's legal standing, we raised several arguments—some of them quite novel (novelty is not a good selling point for legal arguments). Legal precedent held that merely being a taxpayer was not sufficient to constitute "grievance" adequate to bring a suit to correct a perceived injustice in city government. We argued that legal precedent did not contemplate the situation in 1977 of a New York City taxpayer—who was more aggrieved, we said, than any court previously could have imagined.

First we had seen that the city was not accustomed to assemblymen pursuing issues after the first headline. Now we got the impression that the corporation counsel's office (the city's law department) was not accustomed to receiving legal papers which were seriously and studiously prepared, a few novel arguments notwithstanding, particularly in what may have at first seemed to be a lawsuit for public relations purposes.

On April 17 we hit them again in the press. This time, happily, we were joined by the Bronx borough president. As a member of the city's Board of Estimate a borough president had considerably more direct impact on municipal agencies than we did—he voted on issues affecting the agencies not in a 165-member state assembly, but in an 8-member board consisting of the mayor, the City Council president, the comptroller, and the four other borough presidents.

With a member of the Board of Estimate joining our side, our efforts threatened to attract a bandwagon.

After three postponements of oral argument in our lawsuit, the hour of reckoning was at hand.

On May 13 I sat in court waiting to argue the case. Three minutes before calendar call, a messenger came bearing tidings of goodwill from the mayor's office: an offer to settle the case, effectively admitting we were right. Whether this was the result of the nonstop barrage of press releases, City Hall's perception of our threat to pick up more allies, a fear that we might somehow win the lawsuit, the imminence of the auction reform bill on the Assembly calendar, a realization that we were right, or some combination of these factors, we will never know.

But on May 20 we met with representatives of the mayor, the corporation counsel, and the department of real estate and reached a settlement, in which the city did most of what we wanted. We compromised by permitting bidding by owners in arrears only on properties they had not previously purchased at auction. Thus, we only excluded purchasers in tax arrears on properties previously purchased at auction and purchasers with previous ownership interests in the properties they sought at auction.

We agreed to this compromise on a trial basis because the city raised the specter that if the auction rules were made too strict, no one would come. We agreed to readjust and renegotiate the rule if appropriate, depending on its effect on auction participation.

We tried to work out a joint press release on the settlement with the mayor's office. Each side wrote a draft release, and we planned to agree on a final draft. But we refused to hide the fact that the city had agreed to our proposals only after considerable resistance, and the mayor's office was not satisfied with our willingness to compliment the mayor only in that context. So, claiming scheduling difficulties, the mayor's office told us we would just have to go our separate ways on the announcement. On June 6, 1977, under headlines reading "City Calls Some Landlords Unwelcome at Auctions" and "City Shutting the Door on Ripoffs by Landlords," the *News* and the *Post*, respectively, gave us top billing. The *Times* headlined the story "[Mayor] Acts to Cut Tax Delinquencies by City-Sales Rule." Yet even the *Times* presentation couldn't spoil our sense of elation. We had won a clear victory, we thought.

As summer and fall passed, however, we began to hear disquieting rumors that our success was not all it seemed. The city's fear that it would have an auction and no one would come did not materialize. Potential auction purchasers were not scared away by the affidavit requirement. But the affidavit's effectiveness began to come into question.

We had been advised by attorneys in the real estate field that real estate operators, whatever other sins they were willing to commit, preferred to avoid perjuring themselves and, in general, preferred to avoid committing themselves on paper to discoverable frauds. Therefore, we had hoped that the affidavit would have a prophylactic effect. We did not expect the city to review the tax records of each purchaser and thereby catch each perjurer; we had looked on the affidavit requirement as a preventive measure more than as a tool for punishment.

Such hopes turned out to have been a little too optimistic. Gradually reports of perjured affidavits began to filter through to us. We realized that we would have to show the bidders that someone was watching, that the affidavit requirement had teeth.

It really wasn't very difficult to check through the computer records at the Finance Administration to determine the outstanding tax liabilities of landlords or to double-check through the computer records of the Housing Development Administration—primarily geared toward recording building violations, but also listing tax arrears. Nevertheless, the administration, even after imposing the affidavit requirement, was not performing such checks. So we did.

On May 8, 1978, we announced that we had turned over to the district attorneys of Brooklyn and Manhattan evidence of apparent perjury by two purchasers of real estate at the city's auction in November 1977. Each had owed at least two years back taxes on other properties they owned. (By November the affidavit requirement had been expanded beyond taxes owed on properties previously purchased at auction—so long as the property had been purchased directly and not through a corporation or some other entity.)

A third purchaser, a detective on the city police force, had not committed perjury. Instead, he had taken advantage of the remaining loophole in the affidavit and purchased property at the November auction although his real estate firm—but not he personally—owed the city more than three and a half years' worth of taxes on another property.

By the time we made this announcement we had a new mayor. The real estate department was now under the direction of the new General Services Administration, whose commissioner pledged to cooperate with us in rooting out problems and achieving reforms. We had conferred with him in advance of our announcement in which, as we had agreed, we credited him with promising to close the last loophole (through which the detective had slipped).

We first had to come to terms with a serious ethical and political problem. The office of the Brooklyn district attorney had been perfectly amenable to our announcing the apparent perjury. We had turned the evidence over to it a few days before our planned announcement, hoping it could move fast enough on an indictment to join us in our press conference.

But this office found a jurisdictional problem: The sales, though of Brooklyn property to Brooklyn residents, had taken place in Manhattan. Thus, it appeared that the Manhattan DA might have jurisdiction.

The Manhattan DA's policies on press announcements were different. His office argued as follows: What if the subcommittee announces that it is turning over evidence of apparent perjury to us, and for some reason—any of several possible legal reasons—we are unable to get an indictment? Either the subcommittee will look foolish for presenting inadequate evidence and making unprovable public statements or we will look foolish or questionable for failing to get indictments on evidence significant enough to be newsworthy. In general, the Manhattan office felt that the presumption of innocence meant that it was inappropriate to make public statements on possible criminal wrongdoing prior to indictment.

We had a great deal of respect for the Manhattan DA's office, but its position was quite different from ours. Its mandate was to prosecute criminals when crimes were committed; ours was to achieve reforms in government. The conviction of two petty perjurers meant little to us against the need to show auction purchasers, in general, that they could not perjure themselves with impunity: that someone was watching and that they would at least be in danger of criminal prosecution for perjury.

What if we waited for an indictment from the Manhattan DA and none was forthcoming? That would lose us the opportunity to scare away auction perjurers for many months to come. We decided to give the Manhattan DA two weeks before going public ourselves. On May 9, 1978, the *Times* ran our story, "Prosecutions Sought Under Back-Tax Rule."

Meanwhile, the new General Services Administration commissioner, for all his good intentions, had not ordered his staff to check through the back tax records of auction purchasers any more than had the previous administration. The commissioner was still working with the same department of real estate which constantly complained that its lack of personnel made it impossible to take on any new responsibilities, including that one.

But our *New York Times* article, for the impact it had on the commissioner alone, was worth it. He ordered his staff to get cracking on the auction purchasers and refused to take no for an answer. On June 12, a little more than a month after our perjury announcement, the *Daily News* story headline read "City Nixes Sale of 55 Parcels—Bidders Lose 20G." The commissioner had canceled the sales of fifty-five properties from the March 1978 auction because the purchasers had failed to turn in the affidavits as required or, in fact, had owed back taxes to the city. The punishment was worse than mere cancellation—the purchasers had to forfeit a total of $20,000 in down payments for the properties.

The commissioner said, "Apparently these buyers didn't realize that the City really meant business. It would appear that they now understand."

That had been the subcommittee's goal for more than a year. Finally, it was achieved.

In the fall of 1978 we reviewed the results again, and on January 21, 1979, we announced that tax default among purchasers at auction had been cut from 66 to 33 percent. To cut down default even further, we asked the city to close the remaining loopholes we had permitted in our compromise, and it did.

Our reform was not going to solve the problems of housing and real estate tax collections for the city. But it did end the vicious cycle of tax foreclosure, auction sale, exploitation, deterioration, and tax foreclosure again, leading to eventual destruction and abandonment.

Neighborhoods will still decay, and landlords will still exploit buildings. Yet we probably saved several thousand marginal buildings from turning into slums. Instead, they will be sold to landlords with the will and desire to turn them into healthy, revenue-generating assets to their neighborhoods. Most important, we stopped the city from being a party to its own destruction. That, precisely, is what we mean by government reform.

18

Ideals and Limits

I THINK IT IS HELPFUL to maintain a "beginner's mind" in the work of reform. The feeling that you are an expert, that you know just how to do it, is dangerous and damaging. The Zen master Shunryu Suzuki said, "In the beginner's mind there are many possibilities, but in the expert's there are few." The expert is stuck in the rut of his experience; the beginner, without knowledge, is forced to be creative.

In reality the reformer is always a beginner. One of the structural strengths in the role of the reformer is that he or she is constantly criticizing practices of those who, of necessity, are more expert in the practice than is the reformer. It is the very fact of a more distant perspective, of being free from "trained incapacities" or being stuck in ruts, that creates many of the reformer's advantages. Since the reformer is a beginner in every new subject area of investigation, these advantages exist. Yet there is still a danger: the danger that the reformer will come to see himself or herself as an expert in the process of reform and will therefore get stuck in the ruts of his or her own techniques of reform and his or her own attitudes toward reform. This is a way to lose the freshness, the enthusiasm, the crusading spirit which characterize the best reform efforts.

In my own case this has happened at times. Sometimes I have been able to use the newness of subject areas to restore my spirit. Sometimes I wonder whether one's productive years as a reformer are numbered, whether the loss of the beginner's mind is inevitable, carrying with it the loss of the ability to make oneself the cutting edge of the battle for reform.

External realities take their toll as well. When I started out with the Subcommittee on City Management, consisting of nothing but myself and the subcommittee chairman and my tiny group of secret allies, I saw us as political outsiders ready to take on the establishment. My spirit of crusade was at its peak. Although I was a New York State employee, technically part of the government, I could still see myself and my friends as guerrilla fighters of a sort, hopelessly outnumbered, up against the entire political establishment. This was a useful perspective, and it gave me exactly the spirit I needed to do my job right.

The crusading spirit of reform is fragile. In my experience the best reform efforts are accomplished only when the proper spirit is on the reformer. The crusading spirit guided our probes of the summer food program, the fraudulent drug treatment programs, and some of the real estate scams that to us were characteristic of an administration that we were trying to undo. During those sallies the adrenaline flowed, and it was possible to go without sleep almost entirely, if necessary. The urge to advance the front lines of the fray was irresistible.

In later times motivation was more difficult. After a new administration came into power, it was much harder to sustain the same spirit. We had "won"; any additional problems we uncovered would in some sense be anticlimactic. The bad old city administration was out; with our help, the clean new city administration was in. We could hardly crusade against the administration we had just helped elect—especially not when this new mayor and his people were making their own efforts to fight waste, corruption, and mismanagement. So, while we might fight to correct a city management problem that new administrators hadn't noticed, we could not transform a few such problems into an excuse for a crusade against this mayor.

Another problem was our new relationship with the political establishment in the capital. The problem was that the relationship was very good. Rather than fight us, in 1979 the State Assembly leadership rewarded us by transforming the subcommittee into a full committee of the Assembly, and I became counsel to the Committee on Legislative Oversight and Investigation. We moved from a little cubbyhole office on the seventh floor of an elderly state office building to a magnificent suite on the fiftieth floor of the World Trade Center. With my new forty-foot-long office, my huge swivel chair, and my sweeping view across the Hudson to the mainland of the United States (well, Jersey City—but it looks impressive from fifty stories up) it was easy to feel that I had *become* the establishment. It was mighty hard to sustain the self-image of a lone guerrilla warrior.

More subtle factors came into play as well. Some of the people who might have been our targets in the past, who would never have heard of us until it was too late—when they saw their names in our press release—now called us, consulted with us, even before we thought of investigating them. That is not to say that we would fail to scrutinize such people if legitimate grounds for a probe were brought to our attention. It is only to say that the nature of human relationships and human psychology is such that despite our best intentions, it was less likely that we would find ourselves performing such investigations. We were, in some degree, co-opted.

We did not stop performing useful inquiries and exposés. But, for me personally at least, it was less often possible to sustain the moral fervor that had fueled our highly energetic and usually effective efforts in the past.

Within a narrower focus, that of individual investigations, the crusading urge sometimes ebbed and sometimes flowed; it was no longer a reliable motive force. There was no heuristic illusion of a "greater scheme of things," a righteous war in which we were fighting the crucial battles. Rather, we were face to face with reality, the reality that had always existed, but against which now we had no shield of illusion: that we were playing, at best, a perpetual part in a perpetual war. We could lose, by the triumph of corruption and the destruction of representative government, but we could never win.

There was another, more reliable motive force, however, which could be counted on to keep us going: political ambition. While we fell prey to discouragement from time to time, we still wanted to get good publicity. In order to do so, without losing our reputation as serious, responsible, dedicated reformers, we had to continue to do more or less the same kind of work we had been doing. Were we to stoop to mere headline grabbing, the change in our style would be notice-able, and the more thoughtful members of the press and the public would detect it. This would be politically costly, in terms of long-run reputation. So, inspired or not, I had to keep performing investigations. My chairman would continue to pay me, out of the state monies he was allocated, as long as I continued to produce in our accustomed style. Also, after the new city administration came into power, and it became clear that the Assembly leadership would not discontinue our funding, I began to think about succeeding the chairman in the Assembly. Thus, my political ambitions were dependent on his political success and advancement, which was in turn dependent on continuing our efforts.

After two or three months of slogging ahead, doing my job in a responsible but uninspired manner, I discovered the as-phalt scandal. Suddenly I began to realize that we were once again involved in a difficult battle against well-connected op-ponents, that we were, in short, once again involved in a battle that was, to me, worth fighting. The spirit of reform returned.

Were it not for the reliable motive force of political am-bition to carry us through the dry spell, we would never have gotten to the next "up" phase in the psychological cycle. I suppose I would have quit or been fired and gone back to practicing law and making a great deal of money. Instead, the crusading spirit came and departed several more times in the course of our association, and political ambition always kept us going.

Indeed, we accomplished some very useful work during those periods when our idealism was on the wane. A quick press release about inadequate security at a state facility for mental patients resulted in significantly improved conditions. Episodes in which patients wandered outdoors in flimsy clothes to get lost and freeze to death in the snow were eliminated. In addition, the expenditure of police time that had been needed to find missing patients was greatly reduced. Our in-termittent fusillades at the federal Department of Housing and Urban Development, also during one of our uninspired pe-riods, resulted in more responsible administration of its Mott

Haven Houses in the South Bronx, with some amelioration of the excessive rents and terrible conditions there for the project's impoverished tenants. Our exposé of the exploitation of the city lease for an enclosed market in East Harlem by the officers of the market's association helped lead to a change of management in the association that benefited the city and the market's merchants alike. And these projects kept us going until we found more inspiring work.

Our evaluation of the political rewards to be reaped from our system of reform proved accurate. The carrot that the system dangled in front of us was real. In 1980 Charles Schumer was elected to Congress and I to State Assembly. Although the Assembly post that Schumer, our committee chairman, had represented fell only partly within the boundaries of the congressional district in which he ran, the enormous and favorable publicity he had received from our investigation, combined with his active presence in his own district, gave him an overwhelming victory. This was true even though other elected officials represented areas which constituted far larger fractions of that congressional district, and on that basis should have been stronger candidates.

I won the Assembly seat Schumer had vacated for his congressional race. Schumer had run to succeed Congresswoman Elizabeth Holtzman, who was running for the U.S. Senate. Holtzman's "legislative watchdog" image was tested against her more charismatic opponents, Bess Myerson and John Lindsay, in a hard-fought Democratic primary which she won decisively. But the Republican tidal wave that swept away powerful Democratic incumbent senators across the country in the general election in November cost her the Senate seat by a heartbreakingly small margin of about 1 percent of the vote.

Holtzman's persistent and effective efforts to investigate and reform the food and job programs certainly helped build her reputation and made her candidacy feasible. However, the fact that each of us could rationally justify a candidacy for higher office—in Schumer's case and in Holtzman's case risking the offices they already held—points to the political strength we had acquired.

The point of all this is that our system of reform can rely

on political ambition, as well as idealism, for its success. Political ambition can fuel it, and better government can be the reward.

In *The Fortunate Pilgrim* Mario Puzo explained that for the Italian immigrants to the United States, conscience and fair play were not relevant to dealings with government; they "had been born in a land where the people and the state were implacable enemies." So it was for many immigrants of other nationalities. The Jewish Lubavitcher Hassidim of Crown Heights, for example, come from Poland, whose government for the past few centuries has certainly been the enemy of its Jewish people, if not, indeed, of all its people, nor has this changed under the Communists. As with Puzo's fictional Italian characters, transplantation to this happier country did not immediately revise the immigrants' age-old conception of the normal relationship between citizen and government. That conception, at least for their generation, provided no basis for outrage and indignation at evidence of corruption. Sympathies might well be with, rather than against, those who successfully exploited government for their own gain.

In the United States, however, the dominant ethos is one that demands that government be honest. Often enough native American enthusiasm for corruption has existed to hide from view this unique American social premise. However, despite cynical and corrupt American individuals or communities, the American sense of government propriety is fundamentally different from the European tradition.

Europeans have never fully appreciated this and expressed amazement at the naïveté of the American response to, for example, the disclosure of illegal CIA activities. Europeans were surprised that we found such matters shocking; they wondered that we did not realize that government "always" operated that way. Here, rather than learn the European lesson and come to tolerate such behavior as normal, we reacted in just the opposite fashion. With our "post-Watergate morality," we entered into an era of greater than usual public castigation of government dishonesty.

This post-Watergate morality has made it possible in recent years for reform to be as effective as it has been. Ex-

posure of the misdeeds of government officials is a real threat
and deterrent when the public is likely to react with outrage,
translatable into votes, at such revelations. Conversely, reform
is less effective when voters are tolerant of corruption. The
citizens of Boston in the 1940's elected James Michael Curley
to a fourth term as mayor while he was under a notorious
indictment, and he served time in prison during part of that
term as mayor. The citizens of Harlem in the 1960's continued
to reelect Adam Clayton Powell despite his well-documented
improprieties (but finally changed their minds in 1970). The
citizens of Georgia in 1980 gave Herman E. Talmadge the
Democratic nomination for a fifth term in the Senate shortly
after he had been denounced by the Senate for "reprehensible
conduct" in his handling of campaign and office expense account funds. In all three cases some good reasons existed for
the popularity of the officeholder. But whatever the reasons,
the result was that dishonest government was perpetuated.
When the voters so choose, it is hard for reformers to do much
about it.

It has long been argued that corruption in government is
functional and necessary. Chicago under Mayor Daley in the
1950's and 1960's is often cited as an example of a well-run
city under a corrupt government. In Daley's "efficient" Chicago, noted Mike Royko, "the syndicate was still putting
bodies in sewers and car trunks, bombing its way into control
of the restaurant industry's supply and union needs, and had
murdered its way into a takeover of the black policy wheels."
Corruption cost Chicago taxpayers double for parkland purchases; it resulted in major fire and safety hazards in "approved" buildings; it put tax money into the pockets of tax
collectors. But Chicagoans reelected Daley for more than
twenty years, giving their blessings to his type of government,
at their own expense.

When city or state officials select contractors on the basis
of personal connections rather than lower bids or higher levels
of competence, costs are higher. Under the popular but corrupt Governor Huey Long in the 1920's and 1930's, residents
of Louisiana paid almost twice the price per mile of highway
paid by citizens of a neighboring state—and the neighboring
state got wider highways of better concrete, on land that was

hillier than that in Louisiana, where highways should have been easier to build. Out of $3 earmarked for public works under Huey Long, $2 went into the party treasury or private pockets.

This kind of corruption has been defended as a necessary concomitant of economic development. According to the eminent political scientist Samuel Huntington, it is "one way of surmounting traditional laws or bureaucratic regulations which hamper economic expansion. In the United States during the 1870s and 1880s corruption of state legislatures and city councils by railroad, utility, and industrial corporations undoubtedly speeded the growth of the American economy."

Huntington's statement provides a wealth of reassurance and encouragement for glib and shallow cynicism about the role of corruption, but it may well be wrong. Neither the Tweed Ring, the corrupt machine that dominated New York City at the beginning of that period, nor the Black-Horse Cavalry, the infamous state legislators in Albany in those years, did anything to aid the growth of business. They simply hindered any business that tried to develop without paying them off, by threatening and imposing damaging regulations and statutes.

In Cleveland reform of the property tax at the beginning of the twentieth century ushered in one of the best and most productive periods of development in that city, as vacant land was forced into use, builders were encouraged, and speculators were penalized. Reform, not corruption, was the handmaiden of economic development.

In New York City the disgust of bankers and business-people at the corrupt antics of Tammany and its detrimental effect on the city's economic health played a major role in bringing about each of the successful reform periods starting in 1871 under "Honest John" Kelly, in 1901 under Mayor Seth Low, in 1933 under Mayor Fiorello LaGuardia, and in 1977 under Mayor Edward Koch. The reform periods, not the machine periods, saw the most effective efforts to develop industry and reestablish municipal credit.

Some people who concede that corruption does not promote economic development still argue that it is at least a necessary evil to grease the wheels of government. If by this they mean simply that it may not be possible to eliminate corruption, their argument is unobjectionable. But sometimes they seem to mean that it is pointless to try. In response, it should be noted that some government agencies have functioned well after reform campaigns cleared out corruption entirely. The police departments of Los Angeles, Kansas City, and Oakland have been "clean" for twenty years or more, and the New York City Police Department has remained essentially free of serious corruption since the Knapp Commission report in 1972. The federal food stamp program was run virtually without corruption for the first few years of its existence, and the summer food program in New York has been corruption-free, for the most part, after the reforms following the 1976 scandal.

So why is corrupt government, bad government, tolerated and accepted? Some answer that corruption is inevitable as long as people are not honest. In the face of this inevitability, those who give up the battle may wish to concoct a justification for doing so and therefore argue that corruption has a useful or necessary role. The better but more difficult choice is to continue to struggle against corruption despite the realization that there are no final victories. Otherwise, the decay will spread until so much of government is corrupt that it is rendered dysfunctional. This has happened. Chiang Kai-shek's failure to emerge from World War II in a dominant position in China vis-à-vis Mao's Communist forces was in large part attributable to the pervasive corruption that characterized his Nationalist organization. No amount of American aid to Chiang, and there was plenty, could suffice; the more we provided, the more was lost to graft and greed. Chiang's fall was inevitable on this basis alone.

A comparable problem, if less dramatic for the moment, may exist in the Soviet Union. In *The Russians*, Hedrick Smith describes an important reason for economic difficulties in the Soviet Union: the corruption that is rampant throughout the Soviet system of production, with overproduction and underreporting in virtually every factory, and the percentage of the take that is kicked up to supervisors to ignore such abuses, all the way to the top.

Maintaining a society that is predominantly healthy requires that you continually combat corruption, knowing that you will never finally win. In that respect, reform is work for people of humility. Pressuring bureaucrats through the media over relatively short periods of months or a few years can at best move us only a short way to solving fundamental problems—poverty, inequality, crime, injustice. Those who can spend their time only in return for total solutions to fundamental problems need not apply.

Even the elimination of corruption is beyond our abilities. A whole new bureaucracy is the price of having someone to look over everyone's shoulder, and then who will monitor the monitors? Who will guard the guardians? Bureaucratic integrity cannot be absolutely guaranteed, and the costs of very close monitoring are high. Indeed, on the basis of my own experience, I would guess that it is not cost-efficient for most agencies to strive for more than 85 to 90 percent system integrity. If the agency is wasting only 10 percent of its budget, its present ongoing efforts to improve itself are probably sufficient. Anything more would probably cost more than the worth of the 10 percent and in many cases would also take its toll in infringements on privacy and morale.

Furthermore, it is often impossible even in theory to design bureaucratic structures that are completely safeguarded against corruption, according to Susan Rose-Ackerman's sophisticated and convincing 1978 economic analysis of the problem in *Corruption: A Problem in Political Economy.*

So a commitment to reform is a commitment to work without hope of total victory. It is necessary to keep fighting forever, just to stem the tide or lessen it somewhat. This takes a considerable effort of will. But it is in the nature of the American tradition.

It seems pretty clear that our system of reform is designed for use by those who have a commitment to our form of government. Radical leftists (and perhaps rightists) angrily deride the work of reformers as shoring up what they see as the tottering structure of capitalist society. It is only fair to note that the radical often plays a useful role in being the first to recognize ills that others, reformers perhaps, will correct. That the radical identifies these ills to demonstrate a supposed fundamental pathology in the system, rather than to correct them, does not take away from his or her usefulness. Nevertheless, the reformer is committed to movement in a positive, constructive direction, however slow the progress might be; the revolutionary, at base, appears to prefer destruction.

Our political and economic systems are sufficiently flexible to meet the emerging requirements of each new era and can be changed to accommodate those groups that attain enough power to make their wants felt by the society at large. The oldest tradition of the United States is the belief that when government violates its trust, "it is the Right of the People to alter or to abolish it." The people of the United States have not, for the two centuries since those words of the Declaration of Independence were written, found it necessary to abolish their government again. But they certainly have altered the hell out of it. The First Amendment to the Constitution, guaranteeing freedom of the press, codified the principle popularized by Samuel Adams in the 1760's and 1770's that affairs of the state are the business of the people, that it was proper for the business of the state to become "vulgarized"—to become the business of the *vulgus*, the people.

As Alexander Meiklejohn taught 200 years later, it was only with freedom of the press guaranteed by the First Amendment that government by the people becomes meaningful. For how can the people make intelligent decisions if they are denied the benefit of free, open, and public debate of the issues? Only with complete freedom of political speech and press, affording knowledge of what their government is doing, can the people control their government.

If reformers may hope for increased efficacy of their efforts, it is on this basis. Television has made it easier for the public to get up-to-the-minute information on the doings of their elected representatives. This represents a massive change from the days when news, even of major national events, such as presidential elections or declarations of war and peace, could not be transmitted faster than the pony express·could carry it. No wonder that government activities on a host of lesser matters that might have been relevant to the citizenry were not even reported. Unless news items were of sustaining interest, the news media didn't find them worth the bother of communicating days after the fact.

By contrast, today's media, to an enormous degree, permit

the citizenry to monitor, on a daily basis, the doings of its government. This limits the degree to which elected officials can operate without accountability to their constituents. This applies as well to the bureaucrats and other appointed officials ultimately responsible to the elected officials. Exposure of behind-the-scenes activity by reformers is far more potent as a weapon when it can be brought to the attention of the public directly and almost immediately. This is the hope of the reformer.

Our sanguine approach to the possibility of reform through investigation, follow-up, and exposure belies the cynical and defeatist attitude of those who deny that meaningful change for the better can be achieved in government. A thoughtful, pessimistic analysis by an experienced investigative reporter, John Hess, appeared in *The New York Times* on September 20, 1976. Hess concluded that in the usual case, investigations and task forces are publicized, but little or nothing is accomplished. Elected officials entrusted with ultimate responsibility put the blame elsewhere. Regulatory and enforcement agencies claim that they do not have the resources necessary to solve the problem. Hess implied that elected officials, through their failure to set priorities and allocate adequate resources to regulatory and enforcement agencies, are to blame.

While the latter may well be true, numerous case histories refute the claim that nothing meaningful is accomplished. There is, however, a larger underlying truth. Scandal in government is as old as history. Any reformer who imagines that he or she will end mismanagement, waste, and corruption is the victim of major delusions. Furthermore, the same scandals tend to reappear. One of our cases, concerning the price that government pays for road repair, is a standard classic across the country. Indeed, some of the very companies named in our inquiry had been convicted of price-fixing ten years earlier.

It is axiomatic in the trade that newspaper reporters who have covered City Hall for twenty years have seen everything at least once. This is not literally true. There was no summer food program scandal twenty years ago, if only because there was no summer food program then. But certain patterns do recur. For instance, too much power in City Hall is blamed for a scandal, so the agency in question is decentralized. Then, much later, the inability of the mayor to supervise such a decentralized agency is blamed for the next scandal. The first experience has been forgotten. The problem is now "solved" by putting the agency back under central control.

Elected judges are found to be corrupt party hacks, hand-picked by local party bosses in a closed nominating process, leaving the actual election a mere formality. The cry goes up for the appointment of judges after careful screening by distinguished bar association panels. After a few years the list of possible appointees presented to the distinguished panels begins to consist more and more of party hacks, and the "distinguished panels" themselves may be selected with more of an eye toward party sympathies. So the new battle cry becomes "Give the selection of judges back to the people," and we elect judges once again instead of appointing them—putting the decisions back into the hands of those who control the nominations—until the next cycle.

Is the process of reform, then, a process worth attempting? Yes, for several reasons.

First, government functions better when it is under close scrutiny. "Sunlight," said Brandeis, "is the best disinfectant." At least for a short while after the exposé, matters will be improved. Secondly, corruption and inefficiency can be controlled; not cured, but controlled. Government can still operate reasonably well with a small amount of corruption. But even this must be fought to prevent its taking over the entirety of government. We have seen cases in which waste, corruption, and mismanagement accounted not for 10 or 20 percent of a program's funds, but for 70, 80, and in one case more than 95 percent. If such widespread decay is not attacked, it can render government so unserviceable as to bring it to a halt.

What we are really doing is seeking accountability. The government must account to the public for its actions. We are attempting to force on it that responsibility. As the British writer E. L. Normanton concludes, "accountability is a purifying element, a constant reminder that government and administration are not activities intended solely for the benefit of those who practise them—a simple fact, but one which heaven knows, it is easy to forget."

Thirdly, the effort to change government for the better is the oldest American tradition, and a tradition worth honoring. This is a nation that, in the words of Hamilton's first Federalist Paper, was founded on the principle that good government could be arrived at by design and need not be left to circumstance and fortune. The responsibility for good government is ours.

Bibliography

Allen, Steve. *Rip-Off*. Secaucus, N.J.: Lyle Stuart, Inc., 1979.

Banfield, Edward C., and James Q. Wilson. *City Politics*. New York: Random House, 1963.

Barber, James David. "Not The New York Times; What Network News Should Be." *Washington Monthly*, Vol. II, No. 7 (September 1979). On television as a news source.

Barone, Michael, et al. *Almanac of American Politics*, 1974 edition. Ipswich, Mass.: Gambit, 1974.

Benson, George C. S. *Political Corruption in America*. Lexington, Mass.: Lexington Books, 1978. On Mayor Richard Daley and the Chicago police scandal; arguments that corruption is functional.

Caro, Robert. *The Power Broker*. New York: Random House, 1975.

Carroll, Maurice. "Three Democratic Candidates for Senate Agree on Iran and U.S. Aid for City." *The New York Times* (April 15, 1980), p. B3. On Elizabeth Holtzman's legislative watchdog image.

Dinneen, Joseph F. *The Purple Shamrock*. New York: W. W. Norton & Co., 1949. On James Michael Curley's reelections.

Downie, Leonard, Jr. *The New Muckrakers*. New York: New American Library, 1976. On Seymour Hersh and the My Lai investigation.

Feldman, Daniel L. "Administrative Agencies and the Rites of Due Process." *Fordham Urban Law Review*, No. 229 (1978–79).

Gardiner, John A., and Theodore Lyman. *Decisions for Sale*. New York: Praeger Publications, 1978.

Hess, John. "A Scandal Behind Scandals." *The New York Times* (September 20, 1976), p. 23.

Howe, Frederick C. *Confessions of a Reformer.* New York: Quadrangle/New York Times Book Company, 1967; originally published by Charles Scribner's Sons, New York, 1925.

Huntington, Samuel. *Political Order in Changing Societies.* New Haven: Yale University Press, 1968. On corruption needed for economic development.

Leiper-Freeman, J. *The Political Process,* rev. ed. New York: Random House, 1965.

Mead, Richard. "Analysis of Case Closings Under the Face-to-Face Recertification Program." Paper for New York City Division of Policy Research, Office of Research and Program Evaluation.

Meiklejohn, Alexander. *Political Freedom.* New York: Harper & Row, 1960. On primacy of the First Amendment of U.S. Constitution.

Neustadt, Richard. *Presidential Power.* New York: John Wiley & Sons, 1964.

Newfield, Jack. "Running Scared." *The Village Voice* (October 9, 1978).

———. "This Felon Controls the Most Corrupt Union in New York." *The Village Voice* (December 6, 1978). On criminal background of Teamsters Local 282.

———, and Paul DuBrul. *Abuse of Power.* New York: Viking Press, 1977. On the 1969 asphalt-rigging scandal; real estate corruption; mayoral campaign of Abraham D. Beame.

New York Public Interest Research Group. *Take the Money and Run! Redlining in Brooklyn, Two Years Later.* 1979.

Normanton, E. L. *The Accountability and Audit of Government.* New York: Praeger Publications, 1966.

Parrington, Vernon L. *The Colonial Mind.* New York: Harcourt, Brace & World, 1929. On Samuel Adams and the popular discussion of government.

Pileggi, Nicholas. "The Great Asphalt Bungle." *New York* (March 20, 1978). On asphalt connections in the administration of Mayor John V. Lindsay.

Puzo, Mario. *The Fortunate Pilgrim.* Greenwich, Conn.: Fawcett Books, 1964. On Italian immigrants' concept of government.

———. *The Godfather.* New York: Fawcett, 1969. On traditional suspicion of corruption in the road-repair industry.

Redman, Eric. *The Dance of Legislation.* New York: Simon & Schuster, 1973.

Rose-Ackerman, Susan. *Corruption: A Study in Political Economy.* New York: Academic Press/Harcourt Brace Jovanovich, 1978. Economic analysis of corruption in bureaucratic structures.

Royko, Mike. *Boss.* New York: Signet Books, 1971. On organized crime in control of Chicago.

Sayre, Wallace S., and Herbert Kaufman. *Governing New York City.* New York: W. W. Norton & Co., 1965. On the classic role of the New York City Department of Investigations.

Schumer, Charles, and Daniel L. Feldman. "Prescription to End Realty-Auction Abuses." *New York Law Journal,* No. 120 (June 22, 1977).

Shefter, Martin. "New York City's Fiscal Crisis." *The Public Interest* (Summer 1977). On business backing for reform leaders.

Sherman, Lawrence W. *Scandal and Reform.* Berkeley, Calif.: University of California Press, 1978. On clean police departments.

Smith, Hedrick. *The Russians.* New York: Ballantine Books, 1977. On corruption in the Soviet Union.

Suzuki, Shunryu. *Zen Mind, Beginner's Mind.* New York: John Weatherhill, Inc., 1970.

Talese, Gay. *The Kingdom and the Power.* New York: Doubleday & Company, 1978. About *The New York Times.*

Tolchin, Martin and Susan. *To the Victor.* New York: Random House, 1971.

White, Theodore H. *In Search of History.* New York: Warner Books, 1978. On corruption among Nationalists in World War II China.

Whitney, Craig R. "American Outcry over Activities of the CIA Seems Puzzling to Europeans." *The New York Times* (January 12, 1975), p. 1.

General Index

Name Index